Fly Fisher's
Logbook

FLY FISHER'S LOGBOOK

Copyright © 2008 by Marshall Editions

All rights reserved. No part of this book may be used or reproduced in any manner whatsoever without written permission except in the case of brief quotations embodied in critical articles and reviews. For information, address HarperCollins Publishers, 10 East 53rd Street, New York, NY 10022.

HarperCollins books may be purchased for educational, business, or sales promotional use. For information, please write: Special Markets Department, HarperCollins Publishers, 10 East 53rd Street, New York, NY 10022.

FIRST U.S. EDITION

ISBN: 978-0-06-136302-3

Conceived, edited and designed by
Marshall Editions
The Old Brewery
6 Blundell Street
London N7 9BH
www.quarto.com

Originated in Hong Kong by Modern Age

Printed in China by Midas Printing International Ltd

Publisher: Richard Green
Commissioning editor: Paul Docherty
Senior designer: Sarah Robson
Project editor: Deborah Hercun
Editorial and design: Hart McLeod
Production: Nikki Ingram

10 9 8 7 6 5 4 3 2 1

Cover photo: ©Milan Chuckovich/Stone/Getty Images

Collins

An Imprint of HarperCollinsPublishers

Fly Fisher's
Logbook

Terry Lawton

Contents

How to use your logbook

For many anglers keeping a logbook and record of each and every day spent on the water is a satisfying and rewarding activity. But not everyone keeps such a record and may not even appreciate the benefits.

Whatever your preferred choice of fish and methods of fishing—whether you would rather fish by yourself or with a friend—keeping a regular diary or log and reading that logbook frequently will help you to become a better and more successful fly angler. Fly fishing is a sport where knowledge of methods and tactics that produced good sport on a particular river or water can be tried on a different river under similar conditions. This logbook has been designed to help you analyze and benefit from the information that you record easily and logically.

We all have average days, less good days, and the occasional red letter day. And no matter what a day's fishing produces, there will always be a reason, sometimes more than one, why it turned out that way. Regular analysis of your logbook will help you to identify fly patterns and fishing methods that have worked for you as well as weather or water conditions, for example, that have perhaps contributed to a hard day with little to show for your efforts.

Take it with you
Take your logbook with you when you go fishing and if there is a quiet moment or you stop for a coffee, you can make some notes in it. The sooner you can write up a day, the better. But don't worry if you do miss a day. What you are trying to do is build up a pattern and one missed day will not alter the long-term picture.

Improve your techniques and catch rate
Using your logbook on a regular basis should soon start to help you improve your techniques and catch rates, and help identify problems and areas where you know you could do better. This is what the rest of this book is about. It assumes a certain level of knowledge and experience and is designed to take you to the next stage by helping you to think about your approach, tactics, fly selections, and decide if you have the right tackle for your choice of fishing.

The better and more successfully you are able to fish, the more rewarding and fun it will be.

A rainbow trout hooked on a dry fly. Record any small details that might be helpful in the future, such as the precise fly pattern and hook size.

Particularly on stillwaters, what the weather was like, and the direction the wind was blowing before a day's fishing, can effect where you can expect to find fish and so, where you should be fishing.

Just as important as recording fly hatches is to note if there was no hatch, or just a brief hatch at a specific time.

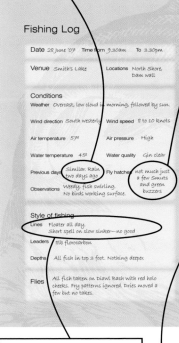

Fishing Log

Date 28 June '07 Time from 9.30am To 3.30pm

Venue Smith's Lake Locations North Shore, Dam wall

Conditions

Weather Overcast, low cloud in morning, followed by sun.

Wind direction South westerly Wind speed 8 to 10 knots

Air temperature 57° Air pressure High

Water temperature 45° Water quality Gin clear

Previous days Similar. Rain two days ago Fly hatches not much just a few Smuts and green buzzers

Observations Weedy, fish swirling. No birds working surface.

Style of fishing

Lines Floater all day. Short spell on slow sinker—no good

Leaders 8lb florocarbon

Depths All fish in top 3 foot. Nothing deeper.

Flies All fish taken on Diawl Bach with red holo cheeks. Fry patterns ignored. Dries moved a few but no takes.

Fish Taken 2 Returned 7

Bag weight 4lb 13oz Biggest 2lb 12oz

Stomach contents Mainly pin fry.

Significant success factors

Most successful method
Floater with small flies that sank slowly. Most fish on top and middle dropper with nothing on the point. Casting to rising fish didn't get a reaction.

Things to remember
Obviously hard on the small fry. Takes came from small flies dropping slowly through the fry shoal. No point trying to imitate them—too small.

Points to take forward
Target fish that have not yet become preoccupied with the fry. Casting to swirls pointless most of the time—better to be outside shoal to try and "ambush" the fry bashers on their way into the shoal.

Other anglers
Very hard for most. Traditional dry fly not successful. Getting presentation spot on was critical. Some very good quality fish caught—3 and 4 pounders.

Additional notes
Later in the day the surface activity stopped. Fish were still caught but deeper, suggesting the shoals were moving to deeper water.

It's worth experimenting and noting what didn't work as well as what did.

Ensure that anything of interest is noted. A pattern can emerge over a number of trips.

Record comments and observations made by fellow anglers, or how you thought they were doing, if you did not speak to anyone.

How to use the information in your logbook

The logbook pages allow you to gather and record information specifically related to improving your success and your enjoyment.

It is important to know exactly when you were fishing. Fish behave differently at different times of the day and in different seasons. The weather has a key role to play, particularly wind direction and brightness. Cloud cover and warm winds can bring the fish on the feed suddenly, but the appearance of the sun can kill sport stone dead. Air pressure has a huge effect too, as a rising barometer generally is good but a falling one is generally regarded as bad news. Keep track and record the weather carefully—it may not be possible to do anything about the weather, but it might influence when you go and what expectations you have.

Location is vital, too. At different times, for various reasons again to do with season and conditions, fish will be in different places. They live where there is food, where it is comfortable to be, and where they can breed. These are not usually all the same place, and it is necessary to know this. The best way to find out is to go fishing, record the results, and build a picture. There is no substitute for knowledge and experience; the logbook will help you build both.

Taking good notes

How you fish—the techniques, flies, and methods involved—obviously relates to the conditions. There is often a variety of

methods that will work, but recording the successful ones, and the ones you feel comfortable with, will save you having to work it all out again. Be precise about this. The fly on the end might not be as important as we like to believe, but if you have confidence in it, because it worked well before, you will definitely catch more fish. Don't rely on vague memories—record the detail and check it out before each trip.

Confidence is the key. This often builds as we fish, and carrying that feeling over to subsequent trips makes all the difference. Note the things that you felt were really significant and what made for a good day. If you have struggled, ask other anglers how they got on and record these results. Then try them yourself.

Note other factors, such as fry hatches, evidence of predators, weed growth, angling pressure—in fact, anything that could be significant. And remember to refer back to the log regularly. It is amazing how quickly things can be forgotten.

A Caribbean Wahoo caught off the reef when conditions weren't ideal for bonefishing. Always be prepared to adapt. It can be a great mistake to approach any water with ill-conceived ideas. What works one day invariably isn't as effective the next, and the successful angler is often one who is able to adjust tactics.

The joy of fly fishing

Why do we fly fish?

There are easier and quicker ways to catch fish if it is essential to catch a fish for food. Fly fishing has a mental challenge that other methods lack, the elegance of a well-executed cast along with the pleasure of making such a cast, the beauty of many of the flies and the pleasure of owning and fishing with high quality rods and reels.

Fly fishing is not always an efficient way of catching fish. Hard days can be very frustrating, but they can teach you a lot. But a day when you catch every cast and end up with a "bag full" can also be disappointing if it seemed that things were just too easy. We should all want a challenge. It can be very difficult to get things just right: When the fishing is hard enough to provide a genuine challenge, but not so difficult that you cannot catch anything. When you have experienced a red letter day like this, it will be a day to remember for years to come.

Get away from it all!

Fly fishing offers you the opportunity to fish in wonderful scenery, visit a wide range of countries, and meet other people with the same interests. This is as true for saltwater fly fishing as it is for freshwater. Fly fishing is all about fresh air, physical activity, relaxing, and getting away from the rigors of everyday life. Standing quietly on the bank of a river or lake, the observant fly fisher can often see all sorts of wildlife around them. Robert Hughes, the author of *The Fatal Shore* and *A Jerk on One End: Reflections of a Mediocre Fisherman*,

wrote: "The best thing fishing taught me, I think, was how to be alone. Without this ability no writer can really survive or work...." Though you can fish alongside a friend, so often fishing is best enjoyed and practiced alone.

Health benefits

The health-giving benefits of the sport have been recognized by the campaign to promote fly fishing to sufferers of breast cancer. Casting for Recovery (www.castingforrecovery.org) is a non-profit support and educational program, and provides an opportunity for women whose lives have been blighted by cancer to get together with fellow sufferers in beautiful, natural settings and learn to fly fish which CfR describes as "a sport for life." The dynamics of fly

fishing can provide a healing connection to the natural world, reducing stress, and helping people to feel calmer. The actual techniques of casting and fishing provide gentle exercise for joints and soft tissue over the course of a weekend trip.

It may be a truism, but there is more to fly fishing than simply catching fish. As your skills improve and your knowledge increases, the sheer joy and pleasure to be had from being on the water and catching fish on a fly will increase exponentially.

Fly fishing can take you to some of the most beautiful places on Earth, from the wild northern waters of Lapland (left) to the idyllic islands of the Bahamas (below).

Fly fishing around the world

Every fly fisherman or woman has got his or her number one dream fishing destination—their dream river or country. Where or what that is depends on where you live and fish regularly. American anglers may want to go to England or one of any number of other countries. English anglers who have relatively easy access to the classic chalk streams of southern England or the freestone rivers of Derbyshire and Yorkshire, may well want to fish in the Rocky Mountains in the United States or Canada.

Belize

Belize, in central America, and the Turneffe Islands is one of the best places—if not the best place—to achieve a saltwater grand slam of bonefish, permit, and tarpon. The Turneffe Atoll has earned its reputation thanks to its superb reef, mangroves, and flats that provide the big three saltwater species with everything that they need to survive and thrive.

Central America and the Pacific

Florida and the Florida Keys, Cuba, the Bahamas, and Central America are the holy grails of saltwater fly fishing. Los Roques archipelago in Venezuela was discovered for fly fishing back in the 1980s and has gone on to great things. Christmas Island, or Kiritimati, in the center of the Pacific Ocean, is reputed to have one of the largest concentrations of bonefish anywhere in the world. Then there are the Indian Ocean atolls of the Seychelles. The choice for the saltwater fly angler is limited only by imagination and the challenge of getting to some of the more out of the way destinations.

England

The attraction of English rivers and streams must be to fish the waters where the arts of both dry fly and nymph fishing were first practiced, to fish the Mayfly hatch—sometimes known as Duffer's Fortnight—and to fish in the footsteps of the likes of Halford, Skues, Plunket-Greene, Sawyer, Kite, and many others. Not only was England the birthplace of fly fishing as we know it today, it was also the country that introduced brown trout to many of today's most exciting and exotic destinations, countries such as Kashmir and Bhutan, Australia and New Zealand, Argentina and Chile, and even the U.S.A.

Mongolia

Mongolia is a country where the really adventurous anglers can have a trip of a lifetime and fish for taimen—a landlocked salmonid—and grayling in unspoilt rivers.

This peaceful view is of the River Kennet in England, where modern chalk stream techniques were first developed.

New Zealand and Australia
The excellence of fly fishing in New Zealand—stalking easily-spooked large browns in crystal-clear water—is too well known to need any further publicity, but neighbor Australia also has plenty to offer, whether it is the lakes and rivers of Tasmania or for that giant of the river estuaries, the barramundi. There is first class saltwater fly fishing in a number of areas around its endless coastline.

North America
The USA and Canada both offer one of the widest ranges of fishing opportunities to be found anywhere. Rivers vary from gentle-flowing meadow creeks and spring creeks, tailwater fisheries, to the big, brawling rivers of the Rockies. If fishing for West Coast steelhead or Atlantic salmon in Canada are not your bag, then there are countless lakes and ponds to be explored.

Alaska can satisfy the needs of many, be they salmon anglers, trout, and grayling fishermen, or after Arctic char and Dolly Varden. Where else can you fish for five species of Pacific salmon as well as steelhead and rainbow trout?

Locations such as this remote Alaskan lake can often only be reached by air. Float planes and helicopters can be chartered relatively cheaply and are usually worth the extra expense.

Russia and Iceland
Russia's Kola Peninsula and Iceland are both best known as destinations for serious salmon fishing but both can provide trophy brown trout fishing. Salmon fishermen who make regular trips to the classic Scottish rivers and rarely, if ever, catch a fish, should go to Alaska or Russia to experience what it is like to actually catch fish. But any trout fisherman looking to catch trophy brown trout should do some serious research into the trout fishing in Russia and Iceland. It is seriously good, and considerably cheaper.

Scandinavia
Scandinavia can offer wonderful trout and grayling fishing high in the remote Arctic wilderness, sea-run browns in the Baltic, and salmon in Norway. In the summer fishing carries on around the clock because it never gets dark. As the Baltic has very low salinity, pike and grayling can be caught along its long shoreline.

Fly fishing around the world

Scotland

Although Scotland is best known for its classic salmon rivers, often with limited access and high costs, many of them offer very good trout and grayling fishing often for a pittance. This can be a great way to fish a classic river. When conditions are unsuitable for successful salmon fishing, trout and grayling will often provide plenty of action.

South America

Argentina and Chile can both provide great fly fishing amid spectacular scenery, accompanied by wonderful food and wine. Tierra del Fuego is the place for enormous sea-run browns and howling gales. The sea trout run to world record size in the The Falkland Islands.

When to go

There are more places to go where closed seasons have been abandoned and so this is not the limiting factor that it once was. Fishing at high latitudes such as Alaska or Arctic Lapland will be affected by winter snow. Heavy falls—in either hemisphere—may delay the start of the season and early snow in the autumn may bring things to a premature end. When snow fields start melting, run-off will discolor rivers and the attendant high water will make them "unfishable" for some time. This is something to take into account. The hurricane season in the Caribbean also needs to be avoided.

Destinations such as Alaska, where there is such a wide range of fish to be caught, can be visited at different times of the season depending on your choice of quarry. Probably the best time to catch trophy rainbows is September when

they have gorged themselves on salmon eggs and the decaying remains of fish that have spawned. Although the autumn is trophy trout time, the grayling will be in good order, too. King and sockeye salmon runs may start in April and May— when flows start to drop and the water

warms up—through to August. Pinks
and coho run from about July through to
September and November respectively.
Chum salmon make a short run from July
through to August, and silver salmon runs
peak in late July and August, and can
provide good fishing into October.

*South American streams fishing for brownies.
An area of the world that provides a whole
range of environments requiring different
approaches and challenges to the fly fisher.*

Fishing Logbook:
Record your trips

Take your logbook with you when you go fishing and if there
is a quiet moment or you stop for a coffee, you can make
some notes in it. The sooner you can write up a day, the
better. But don't worry if you do miss the odd day. What
you are trying to do is build-up a pattern and one missed
day will not alter the long term picture. Regular analysis of
your logbook will help you to identify fly patterns and fishing
methods that have worked for you as well as weather or
water conditions, for example, that have perhaps contributed
to a hard day with little to show for your efforts. Enjoy!

Fishing Logbook

Date   Time: From   To

Venue   Locations

Conditions
Weather

Wind direction   Wind speed

Air temperature   Air pressure

Water temperature   Water quality

Previous days   Fly hatches

Observations

Style of fishing
Lines

Leaders

Depths

Flies

Fish   Taken   Returned

Bag weight   Biggest

Stomach contents

Significant success factors
Most successful method

Things to remember

Points to take forward

Other anglers

Additional notes

Fishing Logbook

Date   Time: From   To

Venue   Locations

Conditions
Weather

Wind direction   Wind speed

Air temperature   Air pressure

Water temperature   Water quality

Previous days   Fly hatches

Observations

Style of fishing
Lines

Leaders

Depths

Flies

Fish   Taken   Returned

Bag weight   Biggest

Stomach contents

Significant success factors

Most successful method

Things to remember

Points to take forward

Other anglers

Additional notes

Fishing Logbook

Date   Time: From   To

Venue   Locations

Conditions
Weather

Wind direction   Wind speed

Air temperature   Air pressure

Water temperature   Water quality

Previous days   Fly hatches

Observations

Style of fishing
Lines

Leaders

Depths

Flies

Fish   Taken   Returned

Bag weight   Biggest

Stomach contents

Significant success factors

Most successful method

Things to remember

Points to take forward

Other anglers

Additional notes

Fishing Logbook

Date   **Time:** From   To

Venue   Locations

Conditions
Weather

Wind direction   Wind speed

Air temperature   Air pressure

Water temperature   Water quality

Previous days   Fly hatches

Observations

Style of fishing
Lines

Leaders

Depths

Flies

Fish   Taken   Returned

Bag weight   Biggest

Stomach contents

Significant success factors
Most successful method

Things to remember

Points to take forward

Other anglers

Additional notes

Fishing Logbook

Date   Time: From   To

Venue   Locations

Conditions

Weather

Wind direction   Wind speed

Air temperature   Air pressure

Water temperature   Water quality

Previous days   Fly hatches

Observations

Style of fishing

Lines

Leaders

Depths

Flies

Fish   Taken   Returned

Bag weight   Biggest

Stomach contents

Significant success factors

Most successful method

Things to remember

Points to take forward

Other anglers

Additional notes

Fishing Logbook

Date   Time: From   To

Venue   Locations

Conditions
Weather

Wind direction   Wind speed

Air temperature   Air pressure

Water temperature   Water quality

Previous days   Fly hatches

Observations

Style of fishing
Lines

Leaders

Depths

Flies

Fish   Taken   Returned

Bag weight   Biggest

Stomach contents

Significant success factors

Most successful method

Things to remember

Points to take forward

Other anglers

Additional notes

Fishing Logbook

Date   Time: From   To

Venue   Locations

Conditions
Weather

Wind direction   Wind speed

Air temperature   Air pressure

Water temperature   Water quality

Previous days   Fly hatches

Observations

Style of fishing
Lines

Leaders

Depths

Flies

Fish   Taken   Returned

Bag weight   Biggest

Stomach contents

Significant success factors
Most successful method

Things to remember

Points to take forward

Other anglers

Additional notes

Fishing Logbook

Date   Time: From   To

Venue   Locations

Conditions
Weather

Wind direction   Wind speed

Air temperature   Air pressure

Water temperature   Water quality

Previous days   Fly hatches

Observations

Style of fishing
Lines

Leaders

Depths

Flies

Fish   Taken   Returned

Bag weight   Biggest

Stomach contents

Significant success factors

Most successful method

Things to remember

Points to take forward

Other anglers

Additional notes

Fishing Logbook

Date   Time: From   To

Venue   Locations

Conditions
Weather

Wind direction   Wind speed

Air temperature   Air pressure

Water temperature   Water quality

Previous days   Fly hatches

Observations

Style of fishing
Lines

Leaders

Depths

Flies

Fish   Taken   Returned

Bag weight   Biggest

Stomach contents

Significant success factors

Most successful method

Things to remember

Points to take forward

Other anglers

Additional notes

Fishing Logbook

Date   Time: From   To

Venue   Locations

Conditions
Weather

Wind direction   Wind speed

Air temperature   Air pressure

Water temperature   Water quality

Previous days   Fly hatches

Observations

Style of fishing
Lines

Leaders

Depths

Flies

Fish   Taken   Returned

Bag weight   Biggest

Stomach contents

Significant success factors
Most successful method

Things to remember

Points to take forward

Other anglers

Additional notes

Fishing Logbook

Date   **Time:** From   To

Venue   Locations

Conditions

Weather

Wind direction   Wind speed

Air temperature   Air pressure

Water temperature   Water quality

Previous days   Fly hatches

Observations

Style of fishing

Lines

Leaders

Depths

Flies

Fish

Taken   Returned

Bag weight   Biggest

Stomach contents

Significant success factors

Most successful method

Things to remember

Points to take forward

Other anglers

Additional notes

Fishing Logbook

Date   **Time:** From   To

Venue   Locations

Conditions
Weather

Wind direction   Wind speed

Air temperature   Air pressure

Water temperature   Water quality

Previous days   Fly hatches

Observations

Style of fishing
Lines

Leaders

Depths

Flies

Fish Taken   Returned

Bag weight   Biggest

Stomach contents

Significant success factors

Most successful method

Things to remember

Points to take forward

Other anglers

Additional notes

Fishing Logbook

Date   **Time:** From   To

Venue   Locations

Conditions
Weather

Wind direction   Wind speed

Air temperature   Air pressure

Water temperature   Water quality

Previous days   Fly hatches

Observations

Style of fishing
Lines

Leaders

Depths

Flies

Fish   Taken   Returned

Bag weight   Biggest

Stomach contents

Significant success factors

Most successful method

Things to remember

Points to take forward

Other anglers

Additional notes

Fishing Logbook

Date   Time: From   To

Venue   Locations

Conditions
Weather

Wind direction   Wind speed

Air temperature   Air pressure

Water temperature   Water quality

Previous days   Fly hatches

Observations

Style of fishing
Lines

Leaders

Depths

Flies

Fish   Taken   Returned

Bag weight   Biggest

Stomach contents

Significant success factors
Most successful method

Things to remember

Points to take forward

Other anglers

Additional notes

Fishing Logbook

Date   **Time:** From   To

Venue   Locations

Conditions
Weather

Wind direction   Wind speed

Air temperature   Air pressure

Water temperature   Water quality

Previous days   Fly hatches

Observations

Style of fishing
Lines

Leaders

Depths

Flies

Fish   Taken   Returned

Bag weight   Biggest

Stomach contents

Significant success factors
Most successful method

Things to remember

Points to take forward

Other anglers

Additional notes

Fishing Logbook

Date   Time: From   To

Venue   Locations

Conditions
Weather

Wind direction   Wind speed

Air temperature   Air pressure

Water temperature   Water quality

Previous days   Fly hatches

Observations

Style of fishing
Lines

Leaders

Depths

Flies

Fish   Taken   Returned

Bag weight   Biggest

Stomach contents

Significant success factors
Most successful method

Things to remember

Points to take forward

Other anglers

Additional notes

Fishing Logbook

Date   Time: From   To

Venue   Locations

Conditions
Weather

Wind direction   Wind speed

Air temperature   Air pressure

Water temperature   Water quality

Previous days   Fly hatches

Observations

Style of fishing
Lines

Leaders

Depths

Flies

Fish   Taken   Returned

Bag weight   Biggest

Stomach contents

Significant success factors

Most successful method

Things to remember

Points to take forward

Other anglers

Additional notes

Fishing Logbook

Date   Time: From   To

Venue   Locations

Conditions

Weather

Wind direction   Wind speed

Air temperature   Air pressure

Water temperature   Water quality

Previous days   Fly hatches

Observations

Style of fishing

Lines

Leaders

Depths

Flies

Fish   Taken   Returned

Bag weight   Biggest

Stomach contents

Significant success factors

Most successful method

Things to remember

Points to take forward

Other anglers

Additional notes

Fishing Logbook

Date   **Time:** From   To

Venue   Locations

Conditions
Weather

Wind direction   Wind speed

Air temperature   Air pressure

Water temperature   Water quality

Previous days   Fly hatches

Observations

Style of fishing
Lines

Leaders

Depths

Flies

Fish

Taken   Returned

Bag weight   Biggest

Stomach contents

Significant success factors

Most successful method

Things to remember

Points to take forward

Other anglers

Additional notes

Fishing Logbook

Date   Time: From   To

Venue   Locations

Conditions

Weather

Wind direction   Wind speed

Air temperature   Air pressure

Water temperature   Water quality

Previous days   Fly hatches

Observations

Style of fishing

Lines

Leaders

Depths

Flies

Fish   Taken   Returned

Bag weight   Biggest

Stomach contents

Significant success factors
Most successful method

Things to remember

Points to take forward

Other anglers

Additional notes

Fishing Logbook

Date   Time: From   To

Venue   Locations

Conditions

Weather

Wind direction   Wind speed

Air temperature   Air pressure

Water temperature   Water quality

Previous days   Fly hatches

Observations

Style of fishing

Lines

Leaders

Depths

Flies

Fish   Taken   Returned

Bag weight   Biggest

Stomach contents

Significant success factors

Most successful method

Things to remember

Points to take forward

Other anglers

Additional notes

Fishing Logbook

Date   **Time:** From   To

Venue   Locations

Conditions

Weather

Wind direction   Wind speed

Air temperature   Air pressure

Water temperature   Water quality

Previous days   Fly hatches

Observations

Style of fishing

Lines

Leaders

Depths

Flies

Fish   Taken   Returned

Bag weight   Biggest

Stomach contents

Significant success factors

Most successful method

Things to remember

Points to take forward

Other anglers

Additional notes

Fishing Logbook

Date   **Time:** From   To

Venue   Locations

Conditions
Weather

Wind direction   Wind speed

Air temperature   Air pressure

Water temperature   Water quality

Previous days   Fly hatches

Observations

Style of fishing
Lines

Leaders

Depths

Flies

Fish   Taken   Returned

Bag weight   Biggest

Stomach contents

Significant success factors

Most successful method

Things to remember

Points to take forward

Other anglers

Additional notes

Fishing Logbook

Date   Time: From   To

Venue   Locations

Conditions
Weather

Wind direction   Wind speed

Air temperature   Air pressure

Water temperature   Water quality

Previous days   Fly hatches

Observations

Style of fishing
Lines

Leaders

Depths

Flies

Fish   Taken   Returned

Bag weight   Biggest

Stomach contents

Significant success factors
Most successful method

Things to remember

Points to take forward

Other anglers

Additional notes

Fishing Logbook

Date   Time: From   To

Venue   Locations

Conditions

Weather

Wind direction   Wind speed

Air temperature   Air pressure

Water temperature   Water quality

Previous days   Fly hatches

Observations

Style of fishing

Lines

Leaders

Depths

Flies

Fish   Taken   Returned

Bag weight   Biggest

Stomach contents

Significant success factors

Most successful method

Things to remember

Points to take forward

Other anglers

Additional notes

Fishing Logbook

Date   Time: From   To

Venue   Locations

Conditions
Weather

Wind direction   Wind speed

Air temperature   Air pressure

Water temperature   Water quality

Previous days   Fly hatches

Observations

Style of fishing
Lines

Leaders

Depths

Flies

Fish   Taken   Returned

Bag weight   Biggest

Stomach contents

Significant success factors
Most successful method

Things to remember

Points to take forward

Other anglers

Additional notes

Fishing Logbook

Date   **Time:** From   To

Venue   Locations

Conditions
Weather

Wind direction   Wind speed

Air temperature   Air pressure

Water temperature   Water quality

Previous days   Fly hatches

Observations

Style of fishing
Lines

Leaders

Depths

Flies

Fish   Taken   Returned

Bag weight   Biggest

Stomach contents

Significant success factors

Most successful method

Things to remember

Points to take forward

Other anglers

Additional notes

Fishing Logbook

Date   Time: From   To

Venue   Locations

Conditions
Weather

Wind direction   Wind speed

Air temperature   Air pressure

Water temperature   Water quality

Previous days   Fly hatches

Observations

Style of fishing
Lines

Leaders

Depths

Flies

Fish   Taken   Returned

Bag weight   Biggest

Stomach contents

Significant success factors

Most successful method

Things to remember

Points to take forward

Other anglers

Additional notes

Fishing Logbook

Date   **Time:** From   To

Venue   Locations

Conditions
Weather

Wind direction   Wind speed

Air temperature   Air pressure

Water temperature   Water quality

Previous days   Fly hatches

Observations

Style of fishing
Lines

Leaders

Depths

Flies

Fish Taken   Returned

Bag weight   Biggest

Stomach contents

Significant success factors

Most successful method

Things to remember

Points to take forward

Other anglers

Additional notes

Fishing Logbook

Date **Time:** From To

Venue Locations

Conditions
Weather

Wind direction Wind speed

Air temperature Air pressure

Water temperature Water quality

Previous days Fly hatches

Observations

Style of fishing
Lines

Leaders

Depths

Flies

Fish   Taken   Returned

Bag weight   Biggest

Stomach contents

Significant success factors
Most successful method

Things to remember

Points to take forward

Other anglers

Additional notes

Fishing Logbook

Date   **Time:** From   To

Venue   Locations

Conditions
Weather

Wind direction   Wind speed

Air temperature   Air pressure

Water temperature   Water quality

Previous days   Fly hatches

Observations

Style of fishing
Lines

Leaders

Depths

Flies

Fish   Taken   Returned

Bag weight   Biggest

Stomach contents

Significant success factors

Most successful method

Things to remember

Points to take forward

Other anglers

Additional notes

Fishing Logbook

Date   Time: From   To

Venue   Locations

Conditions

Weather

Wind direction   Wind speed

Air temperature   Air pressure

Water temperature   Water quality

Previous days   Fly hatches

Observations

Style of fishing

Lines

Leaders

Depths

Flies

Fish   Taken   Returned

Bag weight   Biggest

Stomach contents

Significant success factors
Most successful method

Things to remember

Points to take forward

Other anglers

Additional notes

Fishing Logbook

Date   Time: From   To

Venue   Locations

Conditions

Weather

Wind direction   Wind speed

Air temperature   Air pressure

Water temperature   Water quality

Previous days   Fly hatches

Observations

Style of fishing

Lines

Leaders

Depths

Flies

Fish   Taken   Returned

Bag weight   Biggest

Stomach contents

Significant success factors
Most successful method

Things to remember

Points to take forward

Other anglers

Additional notes

Fishing Logbook

Date   Time: From   To

Venue   Locations

Conditions

Weather

Wind direction   Wind speed

Air temperature   Air pressure

Water temperature   Water quality

Previous days   Fly hatches

Observations

Style of fishing

Lines

Leaders

Depths

Flies

Fish   Taken   Returned

Bag weight   Biggest

Stomach contents

Significant success factors

Most successful method

Things to remember

Points to take forward

Other anglers

Additional notes

Fishing Logbook

Date   Time: From   To

Venue   Locations

Conditions

Weather

Wind direction   Wind speed

Air temperature   Air pressure

Water temperature   Water quality

Previous days   Fly hatches

Observations

Style of fishing

Lines

Leaders

Depths

Flies

Fish   Taken   Returned

Bag weight   Biggest

Stomach contents

Significant success factors

Most successful method

Things to remember

Points to take forward

Other anglers

Additional notes

Fishing Logbook

Date   **Time:** From   To

Venue   Locations

Conditions
Weather

Wind direction   Wind speed

Air temperature   Air pressure

Water temperature   Water quality

Previous days   Fly hatches

Observations

Style of fishing
Lines

Leaders

Depths

Flies

Fish   Taken   Returned

Bag weight   Biggest

Stomach contents

Significant success factors

Most successful method

Things to remember

Points to take forward

Other anglers

Additional notes

Fishing Logbook

Date   Time: From   To

Venue   Locations

Conditions
Weather

Wind direction   Wind speed

Air temperature   Air pressure

Water temperature   Water quality

Previous days   Fly hatches

Observations

Style of fishing
Lines

Leaders

Depths

Flies

Fish   Taken   Returned

Bag weight   Biggest

Stomach contents

Significant success factors
Most successful method

Things to remember

Points to take forward

Other anglers

Additional notes

Fishing Logbook

Date   **Time:** From   To

Venue   Locations

Conditions

Weather

Wind direction   Wind speed

Air temperature   Air pressure

Water temperature   Water quality

Previous days   Fly hatches

Observations

Style of fishing

Lines

Leaders

Depths

Flies

Fish   Taken   Returned

Bag weight   Biggest

Stomach contents

Significant success factors

Most successful method

Things to remember

Points to take forward

Other anglers

Additional notes

Fishing Logbook

Date   Time: From   To

Venue   Locations

Conditions
Weather

Wind direction   Wind speed

Air temperature   Air pressure

Water temperature   Water quality

Previous days   Fly hatches

Observations

Style of fishing
Lines

Leaders

Depths

Flies

Fish   Taken   Returned

Bag weight   Biggest

Stomach contents

Significant success factors

Most successful method

Things to remember

Points to take forward

Other anglers

Additional notes

Fishing Logbook

Date   Time: From   To

Venue   Locations

Conditions
Weather

Wind direction   Wind speed

Air temperature   Air pressure

Water temperature   Water quality

Previous days   Fly hatches

Observations

Style of fishing
Lines

Leaders

Depths

Flies

Fish   Taken   Returned

Bag weight   Biggest

Stomach contents

Significant success factors
Most successful method

Things to remember

Points to take forward

Other anglers

Additional notes

Fishing Logbook

Date   Time: From   To

Venue   Locations

Conditions
Weather

Wind direction   Wind speed

Air temperature   Air pressure

Water temperature   Water quality

Previous days   Fly hatches

Observations

Style of fishing
Lines

Leaders

Depths

Flies

Fish   Taken   Returned

Bag weight   Biggest

Stomach contents

Significant success factors

Most successful method

Things to remember

Points to take forward

Other anglers

Additional notes

Fishing Logbook

Date   **Time:** From   To

Venue   Locations

Conditions
Weather

Wind direction   Wind speed

Air temperature   Air pressure

Water temperature   Water quality

Previous days   Fly hatches

Observations

Style of fishing
Lines

Leaders

Depths

Flies

Fish   Taken   Returned

Bag weight   Biggest

Stomach contents

Significant success factors
Most successful method

Things to remember

Points to take forward

Other anglers

Additional notes

Fishing Logbook

Date Time: From To

Venue Locations

Conditions
Weather

Wind direction Wind speed

Air temperature Air pressure

Water temperature Water quality

Previous days Fly hatches

Observations

Style of fishing
Lines

Leaders

Depths

Flies

Fish   Taken   Returned

Bag weight   Biggest

Stomach contents

Significant success factors
Most successful method

Things to remember

Points to take forward

Other anglers

Additional notes

Fishing Logbook

Date   **Time:** From   To

Venue   Locations

Conditions
Weather

Wind direction   Wind speed

Air temperature   Air pressure

Water temperature   Water quality

Previous days   Fly hatches

Observations

Style of fishing
Lines

Leaders

Depths

Flies

Fish   Taken   Returned

Bag weight   Biggest

Stomach contents

Significant success factors
Most successful method

Things to remember

Points to take forward

Other anglers

Additional notes

Fishing Logbook

Date   Time: From   To

Venue   Locations

Conditions
Weather

Wind direction   Wind speed

Air temperature   Air pressure

Water temperature   Water quality

Previous days   Fly hatches

Observations

Style of fishing
Lines

Leaders

Depths

Flies

Fish   Taken   Returned

Bag weight   Biggest

Stomach contents

Significant success factors

Most successful method

Things to remember

Points to take forward

Other anglers

Additional notes

Fishing Logbook

Date   **Time:** From   To

Venue   Locations

Conditions
Weather

Wind direction   Wind speed

Air temperature   Air pressure

Water temperature   Water quality

Previous days   Fly hatches

Observations

Style of fishing
Lines

Leaders

Depths

Flies

Fish   Taken   Returned

Bag weight   Biggest

Stomach contents

Significant success factors
Most successful method

Things to remember

Points to take forward

Other anglers

Additional notes

Fishing Logbook

Date   Time: From   To

Venue   Locations

Conditions
Weather

Wind direction   Wind speed

Air temperature   Air pressure

Water temperature   Water quality

Previous days   Fly hatches

Observations

Style of fishing
Lines

Leaders

Depths

Flies

Fish   Taken   Returned

Bag weight   Biggest

Stomach contents

Significant success factors
Most successful method

Things to remember

Points to take forward

Other anglers

Additional notes

Fishing Logbook

Date   Time: From   To

Venue   Locations

Conditions
Weather

Wind direction   Wind speed

Air temperature   Air pressure

Water temperature   Water quality

Previous days   Fly hatches

Observations

Style of fishing
Lines

Leaders

Depths

Flies

Fish

Taken

Returned

Bag weight

Biggest

Stomach contents

Significant success factors

Most successful method

Things to remember

Points to take forward

Other anglers

Additional notes

Fishing Logbook

Date   Time: From   To

Venue   Locations

Conditions

Weather

Wind direction   Wind speed

Air temperature   Air pressure

Water temperature   Water quality

Previous days   Fly hatches

Observations

Style of fishing

Lines

Leaders

Depths

Flies

Fish

Taken   Returned

Bag weight   Biggest

Stomach contents

Significant success factors

Most successful method

Things to remember

Points to take forward

Other anglers

Additional notes

Fishing Logbook

Date   Time: From   To

Venue   Locations

Conditions
Weather

Wind direction   Wind speed

Air temperature   Air pressure

Water temperature   Water quality

Previous days   Fly hatches

Observations

Style of fishing
Lines

Leaders

Depths

Flies

Fish   Taken   Returned

Bag weight   Biggest

Stomach contents

Significant success factors

Most successful method

Things to remember

Points to take forward

Other anglers

Additional notes

Fishing Logbook

Date   Time: From   To

Venue   Locations

Conditions

Weather

Wind direction   Wind speed

Air temperature   Air pressure

Water temperature   Water quality

Previous days   Fly hatches

Observations

Style of fishing

Lines

Leaders

Depths

Flies

Fish   Taken   Returned

Bag weight   Biggest

Stomach contents

Significant success factors
Most successful method

Things to remember

Points to take forward

Other anglers

Additional notes

Fishing Logbook

Date   Time: From   To

Venue   Locations

Conditions
Weather

Wind direction   Wind speed

Air temperature   Air pressure

Water temperature   Water quality

Previous days   Fly hatches

Observations

Style of fishing
Lines

Leaders

Depths

Flies

Fish   Taken   Returned

Bag weight   Biggest

Stomach contents

Significant success factors
Most successful method

Things to remember

Points to take forward

Other anglers

Additional notes

Fishing Logbook

Date   Time: From   To

Venue   Locations

Conditions
Weather

Wind direction   Wind speed

Air temperature   Air pressure

Water temperature   Water quality

Previous days   Fly hatches

Observations

Style of fishing
Lines

Leaders

Depths

Flies

Fish   Taken   Returned

Bag weight   Biggest

Stomach contents

Significant success factors

Most successful method

Things to remember

Points to take forward

Other anglers

Additional notes

Fishing Logbook

Date   Time: From   To

Venue   Locations

Conditions
Weather

Wind direction   Wind speed

Air temperature   Air pressure

Water temperature   Water quality

Previous days   Fly hatches

Observations

Style of fishing
Lines

Leaders

Depths

Flies

Fish   Taken   Returned

Bag weight   Biggest

Stomach contents

Significant success factors
Most successful method

Things to remember

Points to take forward

Other anglers

Additional notes

Fishing Logbook

Date   Time: From   To

Venue   Locations

Conditions
Weather

Wind direction   Wind speed

Air temperature   Air pressure

Water temperature   Water quality

Previous days   Fly hatches

Observations

Style of fishing
Lines

Leaders

Depths

Flies

Fish   Taken   Returned

Bag weight   Biggest

Stomach contents

Significant success factors

Most successful method

Things to remember

Points to take forward

Other anglers

Additional notes

Improve your techniques and catch rate

How to choose the right rod
Rod performance and action

How many rods do you need? Will a new rod increase your success and catch rate? Choosing a fly rod is a personal and subjective exercise. There are no set rules to follow, nor is there likely to be one rod that is "best" for everything. But there are certain things to be aware of which should help you to make the right decision. Modern rods vary in length from six-foot small stream rods to 15-foot large river double-handers. They are made to cast lines of varying weights and the AFTM (Association of Fishing Tackle Manufacturers) system is used to define these. The heavier the line, the greater the AFTM number, and typically the range might be AFTM 3 or 4 for small streams, 7 to 8 for still waters, and 10 to 12 for large quarry.

Rod action—fast, medium, and slow

The way that a rod performs is tied to its action and the way that it feels when being cast. Although rodmakers will use different words and terms, rod action can be classified in one of three categories: fast, medium, or slow. Although most

A basic fly rod and the key points to check

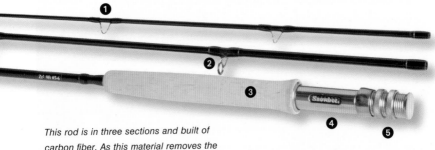

This rod is in three sections and built of carbon fiber. As this material removes the need for inflexible metal connecting ferrules, rods can be in three or four sections, or even more, which makes them much easier to transport.

① Hardened chrome snake rings allow the line to glide through very easily.

② The line guides nearer the handle, known as stripper rings, should be larger and stand away to avoid the line slapping the rod during casting. Silicone carbide linings reduce friction.

③ A good quality cork handle. Check that it does not flex as you cast and that the rings of cork are well finished without holes and rough areas.

④ The reel seat should be hardwood or metal, but check that the reel will actually fit comfortably.

⑤ The connection for the reel should always screw upward as this is more secure.

rods are classified as to how well they will cast a line, it is important to remember that a good rod is one that fishes well, that is to say sets the hook positively and will handle a fish once hooked. Being able to cast a full line is not everything.

Fast

A fast action rod will have a stiff butt section that bends only a little while the flexible tip does most of the bending and flexing during casting and fishing. This action is also known as tip action or tip flex. Whatever the name, it is the tip and middle of the rod that does the work. Fast action rods are good for casting tight loops and achieving maximum distance.

Medium

A rod with a moderate action will be found somewhere between fast and slow actions. This is sometimes described as middle to tip or mid-flex action. Such a rod will have a butt that is neither overly stiff nor flexible and will flex more when cast than a fast-action rod. It may not

produce the ultimate distance of a fast-action rod, but for many anglers it will be a more pleasant rod to cast and, most important, to fish with.

Slow

Slow action describes a rod with a butt section that flexes quite obviously and fully, even during short casts, and a tip that is relatively stiff to drive the action, or bend, further down the rod. This is sometimes called butt action or full flex. This action is most likely to appeal to older anglers who were brought-up fishing cane or fiber-glass rods, rods that many would describe, politely, as old fashioned.

GUIDE'S TIP Which action you choose will be influenced by your preferred choice of fishing, casting style, and your personality.

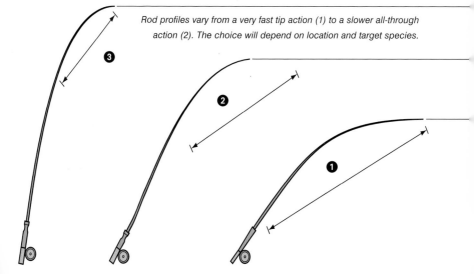

Rod profiles vary from a very fast tip action (1) to a slower all-through action (2). The choice will depend on location and target species.

❸

❷

❶

How to choose the right rod
Rods for river fishing

Fishing rivers with the most suitable rod will have beneficial effects on your rate of success for a number of reasons. Two key aspects are rod length and line weight.

Rod length

A short rod is ideal on small streams or where there are trees close to or over-hanging the water and short but accurate casting is the order of the day. While a short rod is great for precision casting, one will make life very difficult if you have to cast over high bankside vegetation. It will also make it difficult to mend and control your line on the water. Line control is much easier with a longer rod. Similarly, for traditional upstream wet fly fishing, or Czech nymphing, a 10-foot rod may well be best because of the added control this will give you over the drift of your flies.

Rivers are very different in character although the quarry might be the same. The requirements of a rod will therefore be different because accuracy and presentation are the the key. Getting the fly working correctly is critical for success.

GUIDE'S TIP Novice and improving casters should consider selecting a heavier rather than lighter line weight. Not only will this handle larger flies more easily, it will also make casting and fishing in windy conditions that much easier.

Line weight

Line weight will affect your presentation. A heavy line—6-weight, for example— on a small stream will make delicate presentation all but impossible. But on a big river and especially a fast-flowing one, it will be the optimum line weight where longer casts are required and bigger flies are fished.

If you fish brooks, small streams, and rivers regularly with flies of 16-weight and under—sometimes referred to as midge fishing—a 3-weight line or lighter will be required. Not only will your presentation be improved but so will your enjoyment. Your tackle will be working with you not against you. For the angler fishing rivers

mostly, a 4-weight rod, probably between 8 foot 6 inches and 9 foot in length will be the correct choice. Such a rod offers a good balance between delicacy of presentation with enough power to present a fly at distance and the ability to handle larger fish.

Big, brawling Western rivers and similar rivers elsewhere for that matter, will demand a heavier line-weight rod. It is likely that you will need to fish with bigger flies—and for bigger fish—making longer casts, and have strong winds to deal with. For such conditions you should be looking for a 5-weight rod as a minimum, more likely a 6-weight, and some people might even go as heavy as a 7-weight.

Big rivers require heavier gear, often right through to the fly, which may need to be big and heavy.

How to choose the right rod
Rods for still waters

Fly fishing often means that the rod is cast many times throughout the course of a day and the rod is always held in the hand, not placed in rod rests, so it is important that your rod is neither too heavy nor so long that it puts excessive strain on the muscles of the casting hand, wrists, and arm. Some anglers believe that a longer rod will allow them to cast farther, but this isn't necessarily the case. To cast well you must have good control over the rod and be able to rotate it quickly enough to give sufficient speed through the air. A rod that is too long will feel heavy and sluggish. A rod that is too short will rob you of distance and make controlling the drift of the line and the runs of a hooked fish more difficult.

A stillwater rod has to both be able to cast a long distance and be capable of handling large fish.

GUIDE'S TIP A rod that feels comfortable, presents your flies well in the right place and at the right time, and will play a fish well, is the right rod for you, even if you have to sacrifice a little distance when casting.

A powerful rod and associated heavy line is needed for fishing deep-sunk lines when plenty of power is required to hook the often big fish that can be found deep in the water. A rod that will do this well is not going to be a nice rod to use for small flies and light leaders.

The minimum rod length on still waters of any size should be about 9 foot 6 inches, unless you will be doing a lot of stalking when a 9 footer will give you that

extra accuracy that is so important when you have got to place your fly precisely. A fit strong man may well choose a 10-foot rod, but a very young or elderly person or a woman may find this too much to cope with and would be happier with a rod of 9 foot or even 8 foot 6 inches.

GUIDE'S TIP Because the fly is delivered to the fish by the fly line, make sure that you match the weight of line to the size and number of flies being cast. Casting large, wind-resistant flies will require a heavier line than casting a #16 dry fly.

For traditional "over the front" fly fishing from a boat on lakes and reservoirs a longer rod of 10 foot or even 11 foot will give you added control over the action of the flies in the water and especially the top dropper when fishing a team of flies. If anchored, as with the boat in the foreground, rod length is not so critical. But in both situations the angler at the engine end of the boat, if he is right-handed, will find casting a heavier line with a longer rod makes casting over the head of his partner a lot easier.

How to choose the right rod
Rods for salmon

At one time in the United States most anglers fishing for salmon, steelhead, and other anadromous fish would have used a single-handed rod. Long, double-handers were used by only eccentric British fishermen, chiefly in Scotland. Thomas McGuane wrote: "There was a time not so long ago when North Americans saw the double-handed rods used by Europeans as an unfailing sign of their backwardness, their lack of evolution as anglers." Now there is a growing appreciation and understanding of the benefits to be gained by fishing with what has come to be known as a Spey rod and using the Spey cast itself.

One of the best times for fishing for sea-run browns or Atlantic salmon is as the river clears after a spate. In these circumstances, a long, powerful rod is often considered to be a great benefit.

Double-handed rods

A double-handed, or Spey rod, is the best rod for covering large areas of often fast moving water. It is a rod that will master long casts as well as making casts quicker than can be achieved with a single-handed rod. Less line handling is required. A Spey rod will cast a line much further and with much reduced effort compared to a single-handed rod. The extra length of these rods provides a very long lever, which generates high tip speed giving you distance with minimal effort.

It is not essential to learn the Spey cast if you intend to fish with a Spey rod. This cast is the ultimate when there is no room to make a back cast and you have to change direction. A simple overhead cast—when you have the room to make one—will give you great distance when executed correctly. The serious user of a Spey rod will want to learn to Spey cast

to benefit from its sheer efficiency and
the pleasure to be gained.

Shorter, light line double-handers of
around 12 foot for a 7-weight line will
be ideal for any situation requiring long
casts, the ability to mend line and play
trophy fish including steelhead, big sea
trout, and smaller summer salmon at
long range. Big rivers and big fish such
as will be encountered on the Kola
Peninsula, Alaska, or the Rio Grande in
Tierra del Fuego will require longer rods
for heavier lines, up to 16 foot and 11- or
12-weight lines.

GUIDE'S TIP When casting a
Spey rod for the first time,
you must remember that the
bottom hand on the rod does
as much work as the top hand.
The application of power is split
equally between both hands.

*A typical Spey rod (above): 4-piece, 15-foot long,
and with the handle designed for double-handed
casting. Note that the reel seat is downlocking. This
locates the center of balance of the rod directly
underneath the hand when on the grip. This provides
the least amount of fatigue. Generally a lighter reel
is best with a downlocking reel seat, while a heavier
reel is best with an uplocking reel seat.*

How to choose the right rod 137

How to choose the right rod
Rods for saltwater and pike

As well as considering fly size when selecting what line weight to go for, account should also be taken of the species of fish to be caught and the likely size to be encountered.

So, for example, while most tarpon flies can be cast comfortably with an 8-weight rod and line, this tackle would not be adequate if large fish are expected, so a heavier 11- or 12-weight rod and line should be used. The line weight is much more important than worrying about rod length. Almost without exception, you will want a 9-foot, 4-piece travel rod.

The requirements of a pike rod are demonstrated here. Big pike give a slow and cumbersome fight interspersed with short, fast runs. The rod has to be strong enough to cope with this as well as casting large flies.

Pike

The main requirement for pike is a rod capable of casting a big, bulky fly and with enough backbone to subdue a fish that could weight 20 lbs or more. Small pike can be caught successfully on a 6- or 7-weight rod but bigger fish, weighing 10 lbs or more will need a heavier rod, still a single-hander, but at least an 8- or 9-weight. Saltwater rods or a powerful stillwater rod of these line weights will fit the bill well. If your tackle is too light and you catch a big fish that you want to release, you may find that you exhaust it so much if you have to play it for a long time that it may not recover when released. You may need to hold a fish hard to prevent it from getting into snags. A light rod won't have the strength to hold a big fish in open water.

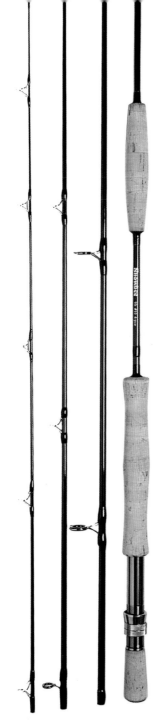

Bonefish caught in shallow water make spectacular long runs, ripping a lot of line off the reel. But a 9-foot, 7- to 8-weight rod is generally fit for the purpose, and will handle most situations.

Heavy-duty saltwater rods

Remember that saltwater is highly corrosive and all equipment, especially rods and reels should be resistant to the damaging effects as well as being thoroughly washed after each use.

Ideally the basic blank should have thicker walls for additional strength and power and the rod fittings should be large, or even oversized, to avoid problems such as backing knots catching as a fish makes long or deep runs.

A heavy-duty saltwater fly rod showing the cork top grip that provides additional leverage when playing fish, and is in four sections to make life easier for the traveling angler.

How to choose the best reel
Large arbor or standard?

For many anglers a fly reel is simply a means of holding the fly line in a neat "package." But for others, the choice of reel is an expression of their personality. While one rod looks, superficially, very much like another, reels can and do look very different. Some of the old classic designs are available, either as updated designs or as new reels designed to look like a classic design.

Playing off the reel

The most important thing for a fly reel is that the line can be pulled off it smoothly, with the lowest possible start-up inertia. A jerky reel or one that needs a strong pull to get it to release line is going to put an undue strain on a leader and if it is a very fine one, it may snap. While this is not so important when you are hand-lining a fish, as soon as you get all your line on the reel and start playing it off the reel, then it is important.

When large arbor reels first came onto the market, there was a lot of discussion, confusion, and disagreement about their supposed benefits. They looked different, cost more than traditional reels and were the subject of much marketing hype. Some early designs were simply not good enough.

Benefits of a large arbor

- The large arbor means that the line on the spool is wound round a larger diameter and therefore the coils are that much looser as it is stripped off.
- The larger diameter means that the line is retrieved quicker compared to a standard arbor. One manufacturer claims that you can recover line in a third of the time.
- A much wider arbor, so less difference in diameter between the outside of the line on the spool and the end nearest the backing, helps provide a more constant rate of line recovery.

Modern reels incorporate simple spool release mechanisms enabling rapid line changes. Most are sold with a number of spare spools so they can be loaded with a range of lines and be carried around with ease.

Although large arbor reels are bigger than "traditional" design reels, the modern, open design and lightweight materials mean that they are not necessarily any heavier.

Cold conditions can cause the line to be stiffer. This causes the "memory," or coils being wound, to take longer to disappear, so a larger arbor reel is a definite advantage.

How to choose the best reel
Drag systems: adjusting and setting

When fishing with very light tippets, the drag—if adjustable—should be set so that it is just tight enough to stop the reel over-running or back-spooling. Many reels for light line weights will have a simple ratchet-and-pawl click drag that prevents over-runs and cannot be adjusted. Such a reel is all that is needed when fishing small to medium size trout streams but do make sure that it releases line smoothly.

A good drag system must be silky smooth with the lowest possible start-up inertia so that you don't overload a fine tippet trying to get the spool running when a fish wants to take line. Sealed drags have the advantage that they keep out grit, sand, and salt, and reduce the need for cleaning and maintenance.

A good drag is essential when playing big fish in big waters. Chum salmon on the Harrison in British Columbia don't offer themselves up easily!

Setting the drag
- Set the drag at the lowest point at which it will stop the spool from overrunning when line is stripped off it. You can find this point by setting the drag at its lightest and then increasing it until you reach the point at which a jerk on the line will make the arbor turn and the line leaves the spool easily.
- Once you have found this point, you can check it by holding the reel in one hand and the line in the other.

Drag systems vary a lot in performance, and generally, the better the reel the better the drag system. Cheaper ones have a habit of letting you down at the critical moment or overrunning and causing tangled lines.

Drag adjustment knob

- Now pull your hands about three feet apart quickly, without upsetting the reel's function, and stop. If the line between the reel and your hand is straight, then the drag is too tight and needs slackening slightly. If the line hangs down in a loop more than about 12 inches, then the setting is too low and should be tightened.
- After each adjustment, check the drag again.

GUIDE'S TIP Don't play around with the drag while fighting a strong fish. You should not need to do so if you set the drag correctly in the first place. If you tighten the drag and the fish stops, a sudden surge could overload the leader.

How to choose the best reel
Freshwater reels

For still water anglers who regularly use different types of line, a cassette reel is an efficient and cost-effective way of having one reel and a number of different lines, each on a separate cassette. Cassettes are less expensive than spare spools and are available in different colors, which helps identify different line types.

For general river fly fishing for trout and grayling, choose a good dependable make and select the lightest reel to suit your choice of line size. If you fish regularly with line weights of between 5 and 7, then it makes sense to have a reel with an adjustable drag system that is capable of dealing with larger fish.

Most reels are supplied with spare spools. It is cheaper than buying new reels, but don't forget that each will require a line and backing!

Backing
Salmon and sea-run browns need a reel with a dependable drag system and plenty of capacity for heavier line weights and plenty of backing. This is even more important if you use a modern Spey line—these are often very long and have thick and long heads that take-up reel capacity. Go for gel-spun backing as you can wind a lot more onto a reel than conventional braided Dacron backing.

GUIDE'S TIP Try not to put your rod down on the ground where mud, sand, or grit could get into your reel, perhaps making it jam or causing excessive wear between the spool and main bearing.

How to choose the best reel
Saltwater reels

GUIDE'S TIP Fishing in saltwater is a problem for all tackle. Although conditions look benign, the salt will destroy reel mechanisms and drags rapidly. Beware not to overlubricate reels as grease or oil getting in the drag can make it slip.

Good drag system essential

The saltwater environment coupled with hard lighting, fast-running fish that put reels under maximum load and pressure mean that the serious saltwater angler should buy the best quality reel that he or she can afford. Reels used for fly fishing for bonefish, tarpon, and permit need a drag that will stop a fish heading for the horizon with no intention of stopping.

You cannot afford to use a reel that is going to jam without warning or even seize up because the main bearing has overheated. Should that happen, you will break your line as well as lose your fish. A saltwater reel needs to have capacity for up to 300 yards of backing. Micro- or gel-spun backing should be the material of choice as you can get much more on a reel compared to the more traditional braided polyester. This is particularly important when fishing with very heavy fly lines that take up spool space.

Reels get wet, and they are designed to be able to dry out, but if used in saltwater they must be thoroughly dismantled and washed.

Lines—the key to good casting
Weight forward or double taper

Modern fly lines are available in a very wide range of styles and profiles. There are continuing developments in line taper, choice of materials, construction, and ways of making floating lines float higher in the water and for longer, and for sinking lines to sink faster.

To add to the confusion, some line manufacturers claim that they continue to refine and develop their lines and make the changes available immediately, rather than launching a new line at the start of the next season. It is all too easy to get obsessed with the virtues of one type of line compared to another. The more lines that you have, the easier it is to get confused and end up fishing with the wrong one.

A good fly line should have a taper designed to suit the weight of line and length of rod likely to be fished with it, rather than a taper designed for a heavy line produced in a scaled-down version for lighter line weights.

Color

What is the best color for a fly line? Do you choose a bright color that you can see easily? Or something more subdued? Guides in New Zealand are absolutely

GUIDE'S TIP Have a flexible approach to each line and really get to know each one well and how it can be used. It is much better to work out what line is required on the day, than to constantly change lines. And much less to carry!

definite that your fly line must be a dull, subdued color that does not "flash" in bright sunlight.

Tapers

The traditional dry fly fisherman will still maintain that the only line to use is a double taper line, but there is a very

GUIDE'S TIP When going for extra distance, many anglers believe that they need to make more false casts. This is wrong. Make too many false casts and you will find that when you make your presentation cast you have lost all the energy created by false casting.

Weight forward (WF) lines have a thicker, shorter section (the belly) toward the front end, followed by a long, much thinner shooting line. These are more popular for larger waters as they can be cast further by the less experienced caster.

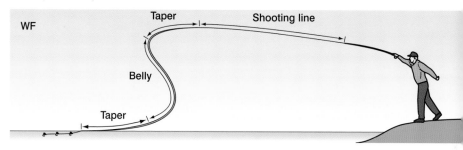

Double taper (DT) lines have the belly in the middle. They are not so easy to cast long distances, but presentation and control of the fly is better. As they are reversible being the same at both ends, and can be changed around as the front end wears.

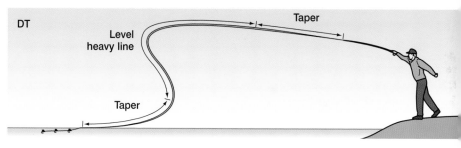

strong case to be made for saying that the best line to use is the one that you can cast best. A good cast with a weight forward line will always be a better cast than a bad cast with a double taper line. Where the use of a double taper line does make sense is when fishing small streams where you always make short casts. After a season's use and wear (on the front half of the line), the line can be removed from the reel and reversed—resulting in double the length of time before buying a replacement line. But

when distance is required or you have to make a quick presentation after perhaps only one false cast, then weight forward wins every time.

One thing that may have put people off weight forward lines was that the early tapers left quite a lot to be desired. But there has been an extraordinary amount of development into weight forward fly line tapers and a weight forward line can have the delicacy of taper of the front-end of a double taper line without compromising casting distance.

Lines—the key to good casting
Floating and sinking lines

Floaters
When a heavy fly is fished on a floating line, it can be fished quite slowly, without fear of hooking the bottom on still waters, because of the buoyancy of the line. You can see what a floater is doing and where it is so much more easily than a sinking line, unless the water is exceptionally clear.

Sinkers
Sinking lines come in a wide range of densities and sinking speeds from the intermediate, the slowest sinking, through sink-tips to lines with sink rates of up to 9 inches per second. Full sinking lines are made with density compensation so that the tip sinks first, getting your fly into the strike zone straight away. These lines are also easier to cast than traditional level sinking lines.

The way that you fish will have an impact on how deep a line will sink. For example you can fish quite close to the surface with a fast sinking line if you limit yourself to short casts. A slow sinker such as an intermediate, cast well out, and left to sink will achieve a good depth, particularly if it is also retrieved very slowly.

Intermediate
An intermediate line will sink slowly and because it is sinking, it will not create a wake on the surface and will be less influenced by wind or breeze causing surface drift. You can now retrieve in a straight line, rather than in a large curve or bow, and your fly or flies will not rise in the water as they would if being fished on a floating line. The latest development in intermediate lines is the slime line, which has a clear tip section. The clear tip is good for stealthy approaches to fish. As they have a very smooth, slick surface coating, they are good for casting long distances.

A selection of reels and lines for still water use. Still waters require a greater range of lines, especially if they are of any depth. Not only do these have different sink rates. but they also form different profiles as they sink, so flies can be fished in a variety of ways.

Basic line densities and sink rates

Floating lines are usually brightly colored although some are of the opinion that this is likely to spook fish.

Floater: does not sink!

Super slow sinker: ½–1 inches per second

Slow sinker: 1–2 inches per second

Intermediate: 2–3 inches per second

Fast sink: 3–4 inches per second

Sinking lines tend to be darker and designed to be less visible.

Super fast sink: 4–5 inches per second

GUIDE'S TIP Are you failing to catch fish because you are not fishing at the right depth or with the right line? Lures are best fished with either a slow or fast sinking line while nymphs and midge pupae are best fished with a floating line.

Many intermediate and slow sinking lines are neutral colors or even clear—as with this "slime" line.

Lines—the key to good casting
Specialist lines

Indicator tipped lines

Indicator tips are better suited to still waters than rivers because when nymph fishing rivers, you want the indicator much closer to your fly, unless you are fishing in very deep water when none, or very little, of your leader can be seen on the surface of the water. These lines work well when fishing nymphs deep or high sticking, when you fish with virtually all your line clear of the surface.

Clear lines

Clear lines and lines with clear tips are popular for stalking fish on still waters and subsurface nymph fishing when the clear, slow sink tip will keep you in contact with your flies. The idea behind a clear line is that it will be all but invisible on or in the water. These lines were developed for lake fishing, but have become popular with sea trout anglers and others fishing subsurface and where stealth is beneficial.

GUIDE'S TIP If multi-number Spey lines are causing confusion, here's how they work. With a line rated 9/10/11 it is the middle number that tells you that the line will best match a 10-weight rod. The numbers are based on a line having the front taper of a 9-weight, followed by the front taper of a 10-weight, and the body of an 11-weight.

Saltwater lines

Saltwater lines are made with the stiffest braided mono cores and hardest coatings so that they maintain the designed degree of stiffness even in very high temperatures. Special coatings are also used to resist the damaging effects of salt and sun.

Spey lines

The development of Spey rods is being matched by the development of specialist Spey lines and Scandinavian shooting head systems. The traditional line for using with a double-handed salmon rod when Spey casting was a double taper line. For many these lines have been

Check your line regularly for cracks. If it hinges when casting, see if the coating has been damaged or even cracked right through. If this is the case, cut off the damaged end and re-seal it with superglue or similar. Sealing the end is particularly important for floating lines. If water starts to seep into the end of the line, it will soon lose its buoyancy and sink.

Modern line developments have produced lines with different densities so combinations of floating and sinkers can be created. A popular line will have a floating rear section with a sinking tip of various sink rates.

superseded by specialist Spey lines with a range of head profiles. It is worth noting that the AFTM line rating system does not work for Spey lines, Scandinavian Spey lines, and shooting heads. These lines are available with varying head lengths and line weights to match the optimum head weight ratings of the rods.

Pike lines

Pike lines are made with a short front taper and heavy front section that will turn over large pike flies. Because flies are often retrieved almost to your feet, you want a line that will load your rod quickly with only a short length of line beyond the rod tip. If you use a saltwater line, do make sure that the coating is for coldwater so that the line will stay supple in cold winter temperatures. A tropical coating that is designed to keep a line adequately stiff in hot temperatures will end up like a piece of hard wire in cold weather.

Another series of lines puts much more weight into the head to enable easier distance casting with casts of 40 yards or more possible.

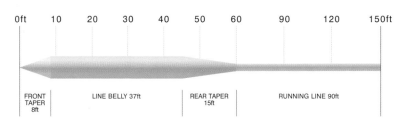

0ft	10	20	30	40	50	60	90	120	150ft

FRONT TAPER 8ft	LINE BELLY 37ft	REAR TAPER 15ft	RUNNING LINE 90ft

This line is a development from the old shooting head idea, but its one-piece manufacture makes it convenient as well as legal for international competitions. The greater distance cast gives a longer retrieve and more opportunity to vary the presentation.

Leaders—the vital link
Which leader material?

Leaders are designed differently for different situations. For rivers and more delicate presentation it will be in two main parts: the leader body which is the long, tapered length fixed to the fly line, and the fine, level section between the end of the leader body and the fly. The leader body, which consists of the butt and the taper, may be a single length—as in a braided, furled or tapered monofilament leader—or made up from a number of sections of monofilament of different diameters. For still waters, saltwater, and heavier set-ups the leader is usually a single length of material.

Tying your own leaders does mean that you can produce a leader with a specific taper and breaking strain. Knots fail and they can catch bits of surface weed and algae. Commercially hand-knotted leaders are still available, often produced for specialist situations. Knotless tapered leaders eliminate all the problems associated with knots.

Pike have a lot of razor sharp teeth. Wire leaders are essential to avoid the fly being bitten off. Note here how the fish is being held—it will be out of the water only for a matter of seconds, but the grip through the gill cover means it cannot thrash about and harm itself.

Braid
Braided leaders have no memory and are very durable, but they have their detractors. One problem with them is that they absorb water which can spray out when casting. As they are durable, they can be fitted semi-permanently to the end of the fly line.

Poly leaders
Poly leaders are excellent for river nymph fishing as they are relatively stiff. They have a loop at the butt end so that they can be attached to the fly line with a loop-to-loop connection and a loop can be tied in the mono core to which the tippet is then attached. Sinking versions can be used as mini sink-tips.

Leader material comes in a bewildering range of sizes and breaking strains. Never use material lighter than is necessary, because broken leaders leave flies in fish.

Materials

There are three main types of leader
and tippet material: nylon monofilament,
co-polymer, and fluorocarbon. Some
suggest that the choice of leader material
does not matter—what is more important
are the diameter and flexibility.

- Co-polymer leaders and leader
  material have high knot strength,
  good abrasion resistance and fine
  diameter. When fine diameter tippets
  are required, co-polymer is the answer
  as the breaking strain for a given
  thickness can be as much as twice
  that of conventional nylon.
- Fluorocarbon is a material that has
  caused many a waterside argument.
  It is made from polyvinylidene fluoride
  (PVDF). This material is much less
  conspicuous in water as it has a
  refractive index the same as water.
  Some makes are more visible in water
  than others, depending on surface
  finish. The material knots well and
  does not decay like conventional
  nylon so you do not need to throw
  away a spool that has been left in
  the light or is a season or two old.
  Fluorocarbon has a greater specific
  gravity than water which means

that it should sink faster than other
materials. This is helpful when fishing
small flies or lightly weighted nymphs.
When used with dry flies, some
anglers worry that it might sink their
fly. But for river anglers who prefer the
tippet to fish just under the surface,
rather than in or on the surface film,
fluorocarbon is the best choice.

*A long fluorocarbon leader left on the water is
in danger of drowning smaller dry flies.*

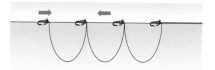

GUIDE'S TIP The fewer knots
in your leader, the fewer there
will be to fail. A simple leader
will be stronger than one tied to
a complicated formula with lots
of knots.

*A good-sized English perch that took a white
lure. These fish are specifically targeted on
some waters.*

Leaders—the vital link
Leaders for river fishing

Dry fly fishing on rivers is all about presentation. This is the time when the correct choice of leader is fundamental to good sport. You need a leader that will turn over and allow you to present your fly accurately and gently. You also want a leader that is not going to be affected by drag immediately. A dry fly leader should have a stiff(ish) butt, a relatively soft mid-section and flexible tippet, which will land in curves on the surface of the river and take time to straighten out, so delaying the onset of drag.

Leaders

When it comes to leaders for nymph fishing, a stiffer leader is required. You want to be able to pitch your nymph precisely and, because you are fishing underwater, surface drag is not such a problem (although subsurface drag can scare fish). A short or medium-length poly leader and supple tippet—co-polymer or fluorocarbon—is a winning combination.

GUIDE'S TIP Using a longer tippet can be the answer when casting to very fussy fish or fish feeding selectively, particularly in slower flowing rivers and streams.

A leader and tippet should be flexible so that they fall on flowing water with a few wiggles to prevent it straightening out immediately and causing the fly to drag. The actual fly line here demonstrates the same principle.

Fishing dry fly for grayling in Wales with a long leader, keeping low and using the flexible leader to avoid drag.

Constructing a leader

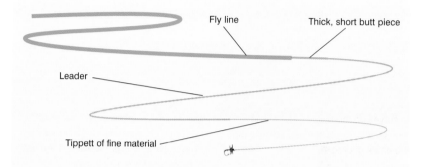

Fly line

Thick, short butt piece

Leader

Tippett of fine material

*The butt section of your leader should be the same diameter or a little smaller than the end
of your fly line, and quite stiff. When tying your own leaders, don't join two pieces of material
of more than 0.002 or 0.003 inches difference in diameter as the knots won't be secure.*

GUIDE'S TIP Choosing a make
of tippet material that comes
on inter-locking spools does away
with the need for a special tippet
material wallet or dispenser.

*A typical river brown caught in quiet water on
a nymph. Note the careful handling, avoiding
direct contact where possible and using
a knotless net. Better still, the fish can be
unhooked within the netting while still in the
water and returned without ever coming out
of the water. When returning fish, always use
barbless hooks.*

Leaders—the vital link
Leaders for still waters

In hot, still conditions fish can be very deep. Long leaders with fast sinking flies on floating lines is a way of reaching them.

> **GUIDE'S TIP** As soon as you find a leader material you trust, stick with it and get to know it. Don't be afraid to go quite heavy on still waters.

Fish have a limited window on the world above the surface, and the higher up in the water they are, the smaller it is. Objects on the surface can be seen in a window of about 96° either side of the vertical, extended another 32° either side for objects beyond the surface.

When fishing reservoirs, lakes, ponds, and other still waters, presentation is not so important as it is on rivers. What is crucial is the way the fly or flies are fished—the retrieve. You will often pull the line to straighten it and your leader before leaving it to fish static or retrieving your flies. This means that leader design and construction can be quite simple. For example, when fishing nymphs or wet flies, a straight through fluorocarbon leader is all that is needed. The weight of a team of flies will help the untapered leader to turn over.

Dries and small flies

When fishing dries it may be necessary to change from fluorocarbon to a good quality mono or co-polymer. Fluorocarbon cuts through the water and can drag the flies under. But light fluorocarbon can be useful if carefully balanced with the flies as it is important to have the leader submerged.

When fishing very small flies, a short length of Powergum in your leader will provide stretch and absorb the powerful lunges of a fish that might otherwise break a light tippet. Tie it in between the top of the main leader and a sacrificial butt attached to the end of the line.

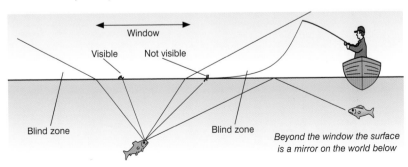

Beyond the window the surface is a mirror on the world below

Leaders—the vital link
Leaders for pike and saltwater

Leaders to be used for fishing for pike and many predatory saltwater species have similar requirements. They need to be powerful enough, with a heavy butt section, to turn over large, bushy flies and be highly abrasion resistant so that they are not cut by ultra-sharp teeth such as those that fill a pike's mouth. Leaders need to end with either a short length of flexible wire, to which the fly is attached, or a length of very high-strength mono. When fishing for pike in particular, delicate presentation is not a requirement. In fact, a splashy presentation can be just what is needed to attract a skulking fish.

Saltwater

A saltwater leader needs to turn over in a straight line so that you are in contact with your fly as quickly as possible. You may not have the time to remove unwanted

slack from your leader. Short leaders are fine when casting into a strong wind, but long leaders will be essential in calm conditions when tarpon or bonefish may be spooked by the line landing on the water. A leader with a butt section of half the length of the leader will help maintain the energy through the cast. Fish a 9-foot leader and you will not go far wrong.

Shock leaders

Trout fishermen may not appreciate the need for a shock tippet when saltwater fly fishing. A heavy shock tippet serves two main purposes. It will, as the name suggests, absorb the shock of a big fish hitting your fly hard. It will also be thick enough to resist abrasion and the teeth of toothy fish. Tarpon fishermen will often use 80- or 100-pound mono as a shock tippet, as anything weaker will not be strong enough for the job.

Not all pike take big flies. This huge 37-pounder took a size-10 booby and was lightly lip hooked.
It was returned unharmed to the water and could easily grow even bigger.

The best knots
The weakest link—tying knots

There's nothing more upsetting than loosing a potential trophy fish because of a badly tied knot. Knots can be a weak link between the angler and quarry because every knot reduces the strength of a piece of leader by anything between 10 percent and 35 percent, depending on the leader material and choice of knot.

Some knots are too complicated to tie under pressure when surrounded by rising fish or in fading light. Fortunately there is more than one knot for almost every need. Choose knots that you know how to tie quickly and correctly and you know won't slip or break under extreme pressure. Using knots in which you have confidence is more important than using a fancy knot that you struggle to tie properly.

If you get broken by a fish, take a look at the end of your tippet as this will tell you what happened. If the end is in a series of curls like a happy pig's tail, then the knot slipped. If the end is clean and straight, it's very likely that your tippet broke.

Always check your knots by pulling them sharply and ensuring they are secure.

A rainbow rises to a fly. The moment a fish takes the fly is the testing time for leader knots.

GUIDE'S TIP Don't forget to shorten your leader when fishing in strong winds and good presentation is that much more difficult. An over-long leader won't turn over satisfactorily when casting into a head wind.

Knots for rivers and clear water might need to be smaller and more delicate. Thinner material will reduce the size but less turns will help—but be confident that the knot is secure before casting.

As a fish is drawn to the net it will often shy away at the last minute, so be ready for the fish to make a final bid for freedom. Many are lost by breaking knots or fine tippets, or hooks pulling out at this stage.

The best knots
Try these knots

Albright knot

The Albright is the best to join lines of different diameters or materials. Start by making a loop in the end of the thicker of the lines and hold it with your finger and thumb. Pass the tag end of the other line through the loop. Pinch the tag end against the other lines and wrap it round all three strands, from left to right. Make at least 12 touching wraps. Pass the tag end of the thin line through the loop so that it comes out on the opposite side of the loop it went through first. Still holding the standing part of the thicker line with your left hand, pull the standing part of the light line, at the same time as working the wraps toward the end of the loop. Once the wraps are tight against the end of the loop, use a pair of pliers to pull the tag end of the lighter line tight. Pull on the standing parts of both lines to check.

Step 1 Make a loop with the end of the thicker line.

Step 2 Wrap the thin line around the thicker line.

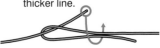

Step 3 Make at least 12 touching wraps.

Step 4 Pass the end of the thin line through the loop.

Step 5 Work the wraps to the end of the loop and then tighten the knot.

Trilene knot

Passing the tippet through the eye of the hook twice produces a much stronger knot, which is why this knot is better than a tucked blood or improved clinch knot. Start by threading the end of the tippet through the eye of the hook, from underneath, twice. Hold the fly with your finger and thumb, keeping the double loop open. The smaller the loops the easier it is to tighten the knot. Wrap the tag end of the leader around the standing part four or five times and then pass the tag end through the first loops that you made. Tighten the knot by pulling the tag end and standing part together, or alternately.

Step 1 Thread the end of the tippet through the hook eye twice.

Step 2 Hold the loops open and wrap tag end around the leader.

Step 3 Pass the tag end through both loops.

Step 4 Moisten the knot, then tighten.

Surgeon's knot

This is an effective knot that is quick and easy to tie. It is great for joining pieces of mono such as adding a tippet to the end of the leader or for making droppers.

Lay the tag ends of both lines alongside each other, with the ends together. Take hold of both lines and make a large loop. Pass the ends of the lines through the loop, making an overhand knot. Repeat. Holding the standing lines and the tag ends, moisten the knot and tighten it by pulling all four ends at the same time. Before trimming the tag ends, pull the individual lines to make sure that the knot is fully tightened.

Step 1 Make a large loop with both lines.

Step 2 Make an overhand knot with both lines.

Step 3 And a second time...

Step 4 Moisten the knot, pull tight and trim.

Tucked half-blood knot

If the trilene knot is creating too bulky a knot at the eye, the standard half blood can be used. It is essential to tuck it finally and trim it close or it has a tendency to slip, producing the piggy's tail. There is some argument over the number of turns, but five is usually fine.

Step 1 Thread the end of the tippet through the eye, and make 5 or 6 wraps round the line.

Step 2 Pass the tag end through the loop closest to the eye.

Step 3 Now pass the tag end through the big loop. Moisten the knot, pull tight, and trim.

GUIDE'S TIP The snitch knot is made by making a half-hitch with the dropper, around the leader. It will tighten after a take.

The best knots
Try these knots continued

Surgeon's loop

Tying surgeon's loops on the end of your leader and tippet is the quickest way to join the two, using the loop-to-loop connection. The surgeon's loop is tied in the same way as the surgeon's knot, but uses only one length of mono.

Make a loop with the tag end of the leader or tippet and hold it with your left hand and make an overhand knot. Pass the end of the double line through the loop a second time. Tighten the knot by holding the tag end and standing line together in one hand and pass something that will not damage the line through the loop and then pull your hands apart. Complete the knot by trimming the tag end.

Step 1 Make a loop in the end of the line.

Step 2 Tie an overhand knot with the loop.

Step 3 And a second time...

Step 4 Moisten the knot and pull tight.

Fishing "the hang" from the bank. Fish will often follow flies and take just as they are lifted off the water and held for a few moments. The upward motion is particularly attractive, and nymphs on droppers allow the flies to be brought through the water layers one by one.

Nail knot

The nail knot is a good way to attach a tapered mono leader direct to the fly line, or to attach a short, stiff butt section to which you then attach your leader using the loop-to-loop connection or full blood knot if you are prepared to sacrifice the length of the butt section each time you change leader. This connection can be improved by making it as a needle knot, with the mono threaded through the end of the fly line with a needle, before completing the knot.

To tie a nail knot

To tie a nail knot, hold the nail against the end of the fly line and then lay the tag end of the leader against line and nail, pointing in the opposite direction, with about 10 inches of leader free with which to tie the knot. Holding everything firmly in your left hand, wrap the tag end of the leader around line, leader and nail at least eight times in close turns, from left to right. Now hold the turns that you have just made, to stop then unraveling, withdraw the nail and then insert the end of the leader or mono into the hole, or tunnel, made by the nail. Tighten the knot by pulling on the tag end, at the same time sliding the wraps toward the end of the line. Finally, pull on both ends of the leader. to tighten the knot fully and trim off the end of the tag.

Step 1 Hold nail against the end of the fly line and tag end of leader, with about 10 inches of leader free.

Step 2 Wrap tag end of the leader round line, leader and nail at least eight times in close turns.

Step 3 Hold the turns to stop them unraveling, withdraw nail, and then insert end of leader or mono into the hole.

Step 4 Tighten knot by pulling on tag end. At the same time position knot close to the end of the line.

Step 5 Pull on both ends of leader to tighten the knot fully and trim tag end.

GUIDE'S TIP When tying the trilene and similar knots such as a tucked half blood or improved clinch knot, it's important how many wraps you make round the running end. Too few turns of thin monofilament may result in the knot slipping. Too many turns of thick mono may not tighten fully.

The best knots
Line-to-leader connections

There are various ways to attach the end of a non-braided leader to the fly line, including braided loops, making a loop in the end of the fly line, or attaching a length of heavy mono of the appropriate thickness. You want a smooth joint that will slide through the top rod guide and that is not going to catch flotsam on the river surface. A connection that will slide through the rod guides is particularly important when you are fishing with very long leaders (frequently on still waters) and you may well have to reel in quite a lot of leader so that you can net a fish.

The best connection will not hinge and will provide optimum transmission of power from fly line to leader for good turnover and presentation of your fly.

In very clear water fish can be easily spooked and even over-large knots and connectors can be a problem.

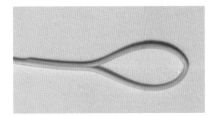

More line manufacturers are making lines with factory-welded loops, which does away with the need to make your own.

The thick end of a braided leader, or a braided butt, can be threaded over the end of the fly line and then glued in place and a short plastic sleeve slid over the joint to cover it. Braided loops are fixed to the end of the line in the same way.

Loop-to-loop connection

This is less of a knot, more a way
of connecting two lengths of line
or monofilament with a loop on the
end of each. This connection can
be undone easily when you want to
change leaders.

Pass the loop on the end of the
standing line through the loop on the
line to be connected. Now pass
the end of the line to be connected
through the loop on the end of the
standing line. Pull all the line through
the loop to complete the connection.

Step 1 Pass loop on the end of the
standing line through the
other loop.

Step 2 Pull the line through the loop
and tighten.

GUIDE'S TIP If you make your
own line to leader connection, it is
very important to seal the end of
the line to stop water getting into
it and reducing its floatability. This
is crucial for a floating line as if
water gets into the end, it will sink
like a sink-tip line.

*A smash take—knots have to withstand the
impact of a strong fish on its initial run.*

Accessories
The essentials

- A leader clipper on a zinger is the number one essential accessory. Without this simple device you can't change a fly or trim knots neatly. Teeth are not a substitute. A small pair of scissors possibly combined with barb flattening jaws for barbless fishing are also important.

A zinger can be used to keep any regularly used accessories.

- A special release tool or pair of forceps (also known as a hemostat or surgical clamp) are essential for unhooking and releasing fish quickly and easily. Forceps can also be used to crush the barb on a hook.

- Fly and line floatants and sinkants come in a variety of forms: paste, liquid, powder, gel, and aerosol. Products in bottles can be clipped to your vest with a suitable bottle holder.

Floatants and sinkants in small bottles are convenient for clipping to a fishing jacket.

- A pair of fishing glasses with polarized lenses is essential for reducing the glare from the water so that you can see fish as well as providing vital eye protection. Wrap-round styles provide the best eye protection as well as reducing the amount of light getting into your eyes from the side.

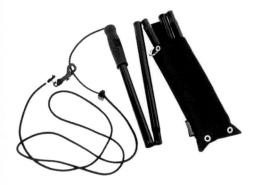

A folding wading stick is so easy to carry with you at all times that it would be careless not to have one when wading.

- A flat cap with a long peak and neck protection is a must for saltwater anglers fishing in tropical climes.
- Bank anglers who regularly make long casts and have a lot of line to recover, particularly on large still waters and saltwater, will benefit from using a line tray. Designs vary, but they will all prevent the line from sinking or floating away from you while retrieving. The next cast can then be made without the line needing to be recovered.

Blunt hooks are one way to fail to catch fish. So carry a hook sharpener and make sure that you use it to keep your hook points razor sharp.

Line tray designs vary, but all must be light and unobtrusive.

Choose a net that is right for the situation. Weighing and measuring nets are great for catch and release fishing as they will give you a good indication of the size of any fish caught. A net with a fine mesh can be used for seining the river to see what bugs are about. Boat fishing requires a net with a longer handle. Attach a floatant device to prevent it sinking should it fall into the water.

GUIDE'S TIP A small flashlight can be a real help when changing flies in falling light or darkness, but always remember to try to keep the glow off the water.

Accessories
Carrying everything

You will still see a fisherman carrying everything in an old-fashioned bag, slung over one shoulder. On a classic English chalk stream you might even spot a wicker creel. Not only are these bags uncomfortable, they are not very efficient. A modern fishing vest or waistcoat is far more comfortable and practical.

Lanyards

For the real minimalist a lanyard round your neck and a small fly box, or two, in a shirt pocket will suffice on a warm summer evening. Though many anglers will want to carry a bit more than can be carried on a lanyard, this approach is good if you are going fishing for a short while, snatching an hour or so perhaps before or after supper.

Modern fishing vests have lots of pockets and attachments for accessories, and some have integrated life jackets.

A lanyard round your neck prevents pockets of vests getting overfilled.

GUIDE'S TIP Keep the things that you use most in the most accessible pockets—not tucked away inside your vest. It pays to keep everything in exactly the same pocket from one season to the next, so you can go straight to a particular pocket and know that what you want is in it.

Vests

When choosing a vest there is much to be said for buying a mesh vest. Mesh is ideal for warm and hot days as it is the coolest. If you are fishing on a cold day, all you need to do is to wear an extra layer underneath. You should not expect a fishing vest to keep you warm. Before buying, do make sure that the vest will have enough pockets and pockets of a size to fit your fly boxes. How you arrange things is not in itself important, but do keep things in the same place. You might keep boxes of nymphs in one outside, front pocket and dry flies in another where they are always quickly and easily accessible. One or two zingers for necessary gadgets—leader clippers, for example—and a clip-on floatant bottle holder completes everything. Boxes of spare flies can be kept in inside pockets, along with other items that are needed infrequently.

Backpacks

Backpacks and
combination
chest and
backpacks
have much to
recommend
them particularly
for the angler who
expects to cover a lot of
ground during the day and needs
to be able to carry food and drink.
They can be cooler to wear and more
compact than a regular vest. Originally
they were designed as a cut-down
angler's rucksack. Now smaller and
lighter versions are available that can be
used either as just a backpack or with a
chest pack clipped on the front for
true versatility.

*The roving river angler, here in New Zealand,
needs to keep his hands free. A small backpack
is ideal for this purpose.*

*A large pocket on the back is always useful for
carrying a waterproof, sandwiches, and a bottle
of water. Make sure that you can get things out
of it without having to take off the waistcoat.
A buckle closure is likely to be more durable
than a zip as well as allowing more ventilation
around your chest on hot days.*

Accessories
Looking after your tackle

This is a beautiful sunny location, but any environment can be very destructive to equipment that isn't washed properly.

The more time that you spend fishing, the more important it is to check and maintain your tackle. Well-maintained tackle will perform properly and will last longer. For those who have to abide by a closed season, that is the time to carry out a maintenance program. If you fish year-round, then you can do it at any time.

Spring clean

- Start by giving your rod a good wash with plenty of fresh water. Use an old toothbrush to remove grime that has built up around the feet of the guides and the reel seat. Screw the reel hood on the reel seat from one end of the thread to the other to make sure that you wash all of it. Scrub the handle with a soft brush and soapy water. Rinse well before hanging the rod up to dry in a warm place and away from potential damage. Apply a dry lubricant to the thread on the reel seat when completely dry.

- Broken, loose, or worn guides will need replacing or re-whipping. This can be done either by the original maker, a professional rod builder, or you can do it yourself if you have the necessary materials. Small holes or a damaged area of a rod handle can be repaired by mixing cork dust in adhesive and applying to the damaged areas. When the adhesive is dry, sand the repair smooth with very fine sandpaper.

- Over time the arbor of a well-used reel may start to feel loose on the spindle. A speck or two of sand, grit, or salt will soon wear fine tolerances between moving metal parts. If the amount of play seems excessive, then it is probably time for a new reel or a replacement spool. As with your rods, an old toothbrush is ideal for giving everything a good scrub. While freshwater reels should be washed and lubricated regularly, reels used for saltwater fishing should be washed thoroughly after every session. Put the reel in a bucket of water or a wash basin or run a hose over the reel for a few minutes.

When you are happy that the reel is clean, dry everything thoroughly, removing excess moisture with a cloth and then leaving the reel somewhere warm to complete the drying process. Give them a good shake to drain any recesses that might hold water. When the reel is dry re-assemble it, using a dry lubricant

GUIDE'S TIP Strip all the line and backing from your reels before washing them at least once a year. Check the connection between line and backing. A clean line makes casting so much easier.

containing Teflon on the main shaft and a drop of wet lubricant such as WD40 on the reel handle. Don't be over-generous with lubricants and grease. Be particularly careful not to get any grease on the bearing surfaces of a disc drag. Check that all screws are tight. If any are loose, tighten them carefully with a screwdriver with a blade of the correct size.

*   If you are fishing water where there is a lot of surface scum, algae, and flotsam or you find that you keep stepping on your fly line, then it is a good idea to clean it more frequently. Lines can be cleaned in warm water with some soft soap—not a detergent—and a cloth, or with one of a number of proprietary line cleaners. When the line is clean and dry, apply either the manufacturer's recommended line treatment, or your preferred make.

Note the corrosion here. If unchecked, this will seriously interfere with the correct operation of the reel.

Take particular care to check the spindle and the drag mechanism.

Keeping safe and comfortable
Clothing, PFDs, and safety

It has never been easier to keep warm and dry or cool and dry when fishing. There is an enormous range of suitable clothing to choose from. Whether you buy everything from one maker or shop around for best value, there are a number points and principles to keep in mind.

If you are going to spend a full day on or in the water, it will pay to dress properly. Start off by wearing a wickable underlayer that will keep you warm in cold conditions and dry when it gets hot. A micro fleece zip tee is an excellent base layer as the zip can be opened on hot days. The high neck covers your neck and reduces the area of bare flesh for mosquitoes to bite. As well as using plenty of good insect repellant, keeping as much flesh as possible covered with long-sleeve shirts and polo necks is recommended. When things get really bad, resort to a mosquito net while fishing, and even when trying to sleep if necessary.

Fishing in New Zealand involves a lot of walking. Wading boots, polyprops, and shorts keep you cool and protected. This angler is about to embark on a trip into the back country—by helicopter!

Life jackets in whatever form are always a good idea–on reservoirs they are compulsory.

Choose a wading jacket that is not going to hinder your casting. If you want a wading jacket to wear over a vest, to keep you dry when it is raining, go for the simplest style, with the least number of pockets. Salmon fishermen usually wear wading jackets instead of a vest, so a jacket with enough pockets is a requirement. A lightweight jacket that will provide protection from the rain in warm weather may not be enough on cold days. A thicker, warmer jacket may be needed for early and late season fishing.

Braving the elements

The main concern of the saltwater flats fisherman is to prevent overexposure to sun and sunburn. Long-sleeve shirts, a flats cap with a neck flap and long pants with zip-off bottoms so that they can be converted into shorts should be the order of the day. Lightweight, quick-drying clothing that will provide good sun protection is widely available.

Breathable waders and a good pair of wading boots with the correct choice of soles are essential. Neoprene or nylon waders will cook you in hot weather although neoprenes are good in cold weather and water. Wading boots must fit well, be comfortable, and provide good ankle support. At one time the only choice of sole was felt, sometimes with added studs. There are sticky, non-slip rubber soles (which will also take studs) that are an ideal all-round choice as they give better grip on grass, for example, than felt soles.

Stillwater and lake anglers, who do not wade, can fish quite happily in a good pair of gumboots that will keep feet dry when standing close to the water or crossing wet ground.

Lifejackets

Boat anglers, float tubers, and those who wade regularly in powerful rivers should always wear a personal flotation device (PFD). Fishing vests with built-in flotation devices are available, as are PFDs that are worn under a vest. Make sure that you buy one that is certified to turn an unconscious body onto its back with head and mouth clear of the water.

The weather can change rapidly, so be prepared for anything—particularly when afloat. These two pictures were taken the same day on an Irish lake.

Keeping safe and comfortable
How to wade safely

If you have never waded when fishing, the best place to start is in a reasonably shallow and slow flowing river, with a smooth, even bottom. Inexperienced waders or anyone lacking confidence in their wading ability should always err on the side of caution if the river to be fished is big and powerful or has a rocky bottom.

When wading always use a wading stick. Even a shallow river can have hidden, unseen holes or underwater obstructions that can trip the unwary. Folding wading sticks, or staffs, are readily available and are so easy to carry that it is asking for trouble not to have one with you. A good wading stick should be strong enough to provide support in a strong current and should have a weighted tip so that when you drop it, the handle will point up out of the water.

A wading stick can be attached to you with either a heavy duty zinger made for this very purpose, or a length of shock cord attached to a wading belt.

Never move your feet before testing the bottom with your wading stick even if you can see the bottom—you might be about to step into a deep hole. Plant your stick firmly and then move one foot—make sure of your footing before moving your other foot.

GUIDE'S TIP If you fish where hiking is a regular feature over different terrain, it could be helpful to have a pair of wading boots with interchangeable soles including cleated rubber suitable for hiking and felt or Aquastealth rubber.

Wading a muddy stream bed can be tricky—boot foot waders avoid the boots filling with mud.

Different conditions require different footwear.
Felt soled boots are excellent at gripping
slippery rocks.

GUIDE'S TIP When the wading
gets tough, get together with a
fishing buddy. Two anglers can
cross a river more safely by
putting an arm around each
other. With three, put the
weakest wader in the middle,
supported by the other two.

Choosing the best flies
What fish eat

Trout are opportunistic feeders and will eat anything that resembles a food item. There are times when they seem to feed on anything going and other times when they can be highly selective. Trout eat flies (mayflies and terrestrials), nymphs, larvae, pupae, snails, shrimps, leeches, small bait fish, caterpillars that fall from trees, and even mice.

Grayling in the Arctic rivers in Swedish Lapland grow fat during the summer feeding voraciously on the millions of tiny midges, known locally as knots, that hatch in such abundance. Trout in these waters grow big through eating small bait fish as they move from lake to river and back again.

As well as upwing mayflies, the thousands of different caddis flies found around the world are a very valuable and important source of food for trout and so are of equal interest and importance to fly fishermen. Because caddis go through a true metamorphosis from egg to larva to pupa and then adult (a mayfly's life cycle is egg, nymph, sub-imago or dun, and then imago or spinner), artificial larvae and pupae can be fished subsurface. Fishing caddis patterns to imitate adults skittering over the water is one time when a dragging fly will catch fish.

Scuds, shrimp, or gammarus—what you call them is up to the individual angler—are always a favorite on the trout's menu. In some rivers you can find more scuds than nymphs and so they are the trout's staple diet. The scuds' curved shape lends itself to being imitated easily by a curved hook and a hump of non-toxic lead weight that gives shape as well as helping to artificially sink it quickly.

USING A SEINE NET

It is useful to know what is in the water at the time so creatures may be examined and imitated. Size is just as important as species. This can be done with a specialised net. Results can be seen in the hand or dropped into a white cup or container.

GUIDE'S TIP As well as everyone being aware of the importance of caddis, river anglers should be aware of the number of midge pupae that trout eat. Because they are so small, fish have to eat a lot of them and a well-presented imitation can be very effective when fish are feeding on pupae.

Natural and imitation mayfly and daddy longlegs.

SPOONING A FISH

Examining stomach contents of a caught fish can reveal exactly what it will have been eating. Once the fish is dispatched gently push a marrow spoon into its mouth and down into the stomach.

Carefully withdraw the spoon and note the food items and their position. The nearer the point of the spoon, the earlier the item was eaten. Also look to see if anything is still alive or if it has started to be digested. This indicates how long ago it was swallowed. Many creatures will still be moving, indicating what the fish might have been looking for when it was caught.

General information can be gained immediately from spooning a fish. Here, nymphs of various sizes are present, along with a large quantity of water fleas (daphnia)—a staple diet of the still-water trout.

Choosing the best flies
Matching the hatch

Match the hatch, or select a generic pattern? Are the fish that you can see rising feeding selectively or opportunistically? Always fish a searching dry fly when there is no obvious hatch but conditions are such that a fish could expect to see a floating fly. Change to a hatch-matching imitation when there is a hatch on and you have something to match. If you can see fish nymphing, then that's the tactic to use. But be prepared to change to an emerger as the hatch progresses and, if that stage comes to an end, then a dry.

If you see the odd fly on the water and you can see fish taking nymphs, do you wait for the hatch to develop so that you can fish on a hatch-matcher dry fly? If you do not fish a nymph, you may end up with no fish because the hatch never materialized. But in mid-season when hatches are usually reliable it can be worth waiting for the hatch and the big fish to join in. Starting fishing too soon runs the risk of catching small fish and frightening big fish or putting a trophy fish down and off its food.

When there is more than one variety of mayfly on the water, steady, repeat rises in the same location are indicative of a fish feeding selectively. Selective feeders are happy to wait for the right mayfly to come within range, rather than keeping moving about grabbing everything and anything that passes. Selectivity makes sense because a trout needs to consume the maximum amount of food with the minimum expenditure of energy. A porpoising trout—head and tail rises—is often keyed in to feeding on emergers. Casting a dry fly to such a fish is unlikely to catch it because it is expecting to find its next morsel of food underwater, not floating on the surface.

Are the fish feeding on what you think they are? Is a heavy hatch of one fly masking the fact that the fish are taking something else, or perhaps feeding on emerging caddis pupae rather than the adults? As well as looking and observing what is happening, it is important to match the actual phase of a hatch.

Three Irish duckfly patterns from current Irish international Sam McGowan. All intended to imitate the natural, but varying slightly in an attempt to exaggerate key features and make it stand out from the real thing.

The right fly might be an exaggeration of the natural insect. This grayling has taken a pink bug, which is obviously something it thinks it can eat. Presentation and getting the right depth and speed is vital.

Different conditions require different flies. A good wave with a fair "chop" on the water will cause fish to swim at higher levels. They could be just under, or even on, the surface. Bigger flies, often pulled through the upper layers can be used—especially if the weather is dull. A flat calm in bright weather might suggest small nymph patterns.

Choosing the best flies
A basic fly box

If you are not going to spend all your time agonizing over whether or not you have got the right fly on the end of your line, hunting through fly box after fly box for that elusive "killer" pattern, it makes sense to limit your selection of flies to patterns that you know will catch fish for you most of the time and on most of the waters that you fish regularly. This will mean that you can fish your flies with confidence.

Don't carry too many flies

How you select and organize your flies will be influenced by your approach to fly fishing—do you always want to be able to cover every eventuality? Do you like making things complicated? If you like a complex, scientific approach and carry boxes of nymphs, larvae, and pupae, emergers, stillborns, upwings, and spent patterns, or prefer a simpler approach with a box of mixed nymphs and another of mixed dries, and perhaps a box of "must have" patterns, there are some essential patterns that every angler should carry, regardless of where they live or fish. These are basic, go-to flies that will catch fish around the world— flies that you have got confidence in fishing either because you know they

These two fly boxes show how different waters require different patterns. The small river nymphs are purely imitative compared with the gaudy attractors used for rainbows on lakes, which are not meant to look edible at all but purely initiate a response.

work for you or they have a history of catching fish. Flies that represent a wide range of naturals, or that can be fished in different ways to represent different food forms, should be the basis of a good fly box, whether dry flies, nymphs, or streamers. Your choice of flies should be based on where you live, the waters you

GUIDE'S TIP Combinations of attractors and nymphs can be used as in the "washing line." Here it will be a coral booby on the top dropper, two diawl bachs in the middle, and a black booby on the point.

fish and your preferred way of fishing.
As well as artificials to match specific
naturals or stages of a hatch, a selection
of searching patterns will always pay
dividends. You can use them to fish the
water in expectation of getting an offer
and when you are uncertain what is the
correct artificial to fish. Select searching
patterns that inspire confidence. Good
searching patterns have one or more
triggers in their design.

Reviving old flies

Badly chewed and really worn flies
that have passed their usefulness are
probably best disposed of. Flies that
have been squashed or that have
bedraggled hackles can often be revived
by steaming them. To do this you need
a pair of forceps or needle-nose pliers
and a kettle or saucepan of boiling water.
Simply hold each fly in turn in the steam
for about 30 seconds, fluff up the hackles
with your fingers and then let them dry.
If necessary repeat the steam treatment.
While sorting out your fly boxes, it is
also sensible to check hook points and
sharpen any that are blunt or damaged.

*This fly box contains a typical collection of dry
flies for river or stillwater.*

Choosing the best flies
Basic trout patterns

With the huge permutation of conditions, seasons, locations, and weather, fly selection is critical. Key to success is using the right fly and presenting it appropriately. For all styles of fishing, flies fall into basic categories and it is important to refresh your understanding of these before learning how subtle variations on these themes make all the difference.

Lures
We know that fish will chase flies that are designed to trigger their predatory instincts. Flies that do this are called lures, and are usually designed to stimulate an attack rather than imitate any particular food item. A good example is the Sparkler (above)—a simple but very effective lure.

Other lures are tied using bright, flashy mobile materials, which can work if fished slowly, allowing the materials to wiggle and gyrate enticingly in the water. One that pretends to be a small fish is the Minkie (right).

Depth and speed
Depth is critical with lures, so starting with a medium sink line, such as a DI3, cast out then count to five, followed by five steady pulls. If nothing happens then try counting to 10, and then 15, and so on. If a fish takes the fly you will know exactly how to retrieve again to reach the feeding depth.

Nymphs and buzzers
The most common insect food items are the pupal stages of midges known to anglers as buzzers. There are thousands of species of these, so they are tied in all colors and patterns. But the black with an orange thorax, pearly thorax cover, and silver rib is a very good all rounder. The Epoxy Buzzer is coated with clear epoxy resin to make it sink quickly (below).

Dry flies and emergers

You have almost certainly discovered that, when the weather is mild and overcast, fish will move up in the water and if food is present they will feed off the surface or just below it.

This presents you with a variety of opportunities, particularly with a dry fly. The word "dry" suggests a fly sitting on top of the water imitating an insect sitting on the surface. This could be a terrestrial blown on to the water, or, more likely, a nymph breaking out of its pupal shuck to become a fully developed adult. As they wait for their wings to dry, they are vulnerable to hungry fish below.

A classic dry fly would be the Adams (above), which has a bushy dressing designed to hold a special flotant and keep it on the water. The emerging adult can be mimicked with patterns such as the Shipman's Buzzer (below), which sits in the film.

When fish are feeding on fry they often swim into the shoals, "bashing" them. The dead ones are then mopped up. A Deer-hair Fry (below), tied with shaped deer hair and colored with felt pens, will often take these fish.

Boobies and muddlers

Deer hair is hollow and naturally floats. When tied tightly and shaped around a hook it produces a highly buoyant and bulky fly that will create a fish-attractive wake when pulled quickly through the surface. The famous Muddler Minnow (below) was designed for this.

Modern materials achieve the same effect but much more easily. A popular fly using plastic foam is the Booby. Designed originally to fish with sinking lines on short leaders, and float just off the bottom, they are now used on all lines, and at all depths and speeds of retrieve. Popular colors include the Orange Booby (below), white, black, and coral pink.

If all else fails, a standard small nymph such as a Pheasant Tail or Hare's Ear (below), fished slowly on a floater, will take fish all year round.

Choosing the best flies
River trout flies

The box above contains a mix of river flies, mainly bugs. Most are weighted with lead, titanium, or gold beads to cater for different river conditions—note the predominance of pink.

These three flies are typical English river patterns. The florescent pink wing on the dry is a sight indicator.

This is an example of traditional and classic river dry, the Royal Wulff, which was first tied by the well-known angler Lee Wulff.

This box of river dry flies contains general patterns such as Adams and parachute patterns, where size can be critical. Bigger sizes imitate terrestrial and wind-blown insects as well as larger waterborne flies.

This modern pattern uses cul de canard feathers from around the preen gland of a duck.

The Peeping Caddis is designed to resemble a cased larva crawling along the bottom.

Caddis fly larvae and adults are all fairly similar, but there are many species. The larva builds itself a protective case of stones or detritus and is imitated by a number of patterns. The adult is less favored by fish, but is occasionally taken and various general and emerger patterns are used when they are on the menu.

Choosing the best flies
Salmon flies

Salmon flies are tied worldwide in a variety of styles and many are based on age-old patterns. The exotic feathers are thankfully no longer used, but modern dyes and materials have not limited the inventiveness of the modern flydressers. Hairwing flies tend now to dominate and this is a small selection.

The Garry is intended for use in summer in low, clear water conditions. These hairwing patterns are tied using bucktail, which is durable and does not fall apart with rough handling. The flies generally imitate small fish, but probably simply initiate an aggressive response from the salmon that do not feed in freshwater.

The Blue Charm is another summer fly and a standard Atlantic salmon pattern.

Ally's Shrimp is probably the favorite choice for Atlantic salmon anglers in the U.K. This again uses dyed bucktail—orange, although other colors are now popular.

The Alaskabou (below) is particularly designed for Pacific salmon and steelhead. The dyed leg feathers of a turkey substitute for marabou feathers.

The Stoat's Tail (above) was named after the material used in the original dressing but this has now been replaced by the ubiquitous bucktail.

Choosing the best flies
Saltwater and pike flies

Pike flies can all be very simple. All that is required is that they seduce a pike into thinking that it is about to miss a good meal if it does not eat your fly. Poppers are good for surface fishing, particularly where there is weed. Clouser deep minnows, zonkers and big, flashy streamers can all be successful.

If you tie your own flies, they can be tied on sea fishing hooks such as the Aberdeen hook or stainless steel saltwater fly fishing hooks and there are some special pike hooks on the market. The size of the finished fly is more important than color. Weed guards are recommended for shallow, weedy waters. Pike usually attack their quarry side-on, which can make it easier to set the hook in the scissors of its jaws where you can be sure of a solid hook-up, with a sideways strike. Striking upward may mean that you try to drive the hook into the bony roof of its mouth.

Small pike or jacks can be great sport—often when other species are reluctant to feed. But feeding spells can happen suddenly and then stop as though a switch has been thrown.

Pike flies in the water, showing how the colors remain bright, goading the pike into attacking.

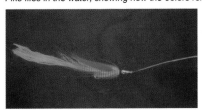

Reading the water What are the conditions telling you?

Virtually every angler wants to get started fishing as quickly as possible and there are times when that very first rise of the day may be the last that you see for some time. However, try to be patient and have a look around. Spend some time working out exactly what you need to do to catch fish. This thinking time is very important. Having decided on what to do, approach the water and the situation of that day positively.

Unfamiliar territory

When approaching a new stretch of water, the first things to look for are structures in the water. Fish have simple requirements

An American stream in prime condition. Try and work out exactly where fish will be lying and how to get a fly presented to them in as natural a way as possible.

for a long and happy life: They need a plentiful supply of food, shelter from predators, and somewhere to live that requires the minimum expenditure of energy. A structure such as a fallen tree will supply these requirements. Rocks and boulders also provide good lies for fish as there is a low pressure area immediately in front of a boulder: Little energy is required to stay in the low pressure area.

Reservoir and stillwater anglers should make use of low water levels to explore the shore that will be exposed when levels drop dramatically. Now is the time that you can find old field drains or streams, the remains of hedges or trees, stone or brick walls, drop-offs, and anything else that affects the depth and contours and could provide a source of food or shelter for fish.

Time spent walking carefully and slowly along a river bank—always keeping well back from the water and out of sight of fish—will tell you what you can expect "round the next bend." The clearer and shallower the water the more care you must take to avoid being seen by fish. Another reason for not walking close to the water's edge is you do not want to spoil the fishing for other anglers. There is perhaps nothing more annoying than carefully and patiently working your way into position to have a shot at a trophy fish and then another angler suddenly marches past you and spooks your fish.

Waiting for the perfect conditions is not always possible. Low water as in this South African stream means extra stealth is required.

New Zealand is a paradise for the fly fisher. But conditions have to be right to catch fish like this.

Reading the water
How to see fish

Try and imagine what things look like viewed from below the water. Fish look up and down, and their field of vision is dictated by their position in the water and its clarity.

Shadows can often be the first sign of a fish in a river, particularly on sunny days. Was that flash caused by a swirling fish catching a nymph or hatching fly?

River anglers and particularly nymph fishermen stalking or casting to sighted, feeding fish are more interested in being able to see fish in the water than most still-water anglers.

As not all rivers and streams are crystal clear so that fish can be spotted easily, it helps to know where to expect to see or find fish. When looking for fish in a river you must look through the water, not just at the surface of the river. Polarized glasses cut glare and make it easier to see into water. Tell-tale signs to look for include something that looks just that bit different from the surroundings— is something moving faster or slower than a near-by weed? Is that straight line the tail fin of a trout? Everything else looks soft and fluid. Is that darker patch of sand the shadow of a fish?

Seeing fish in broken water or where the surface is ruffled by the breeze is not as easy as in smooth water. But even on windy days you will find lulls and smooth areas where you have a better chance of looking into and through the water.

Bonefish in Caribbean shallows (above) and trout in a Montana stream (left)—in both these situations it can be tricky to spot the actual fish. It is easier, in fact, to see the fish's shadow.

The worst conditions for seeing fish are dull, windy days, when there is no sun to help, and the ripples make looking into the river all but impossible.

To have the best chance of seeing a fish in a river may mean changing your position to one where you are perhaps a bit higher or the angle of the sun is more helpful. Don't forget your shadow on sunny days, which may fall across the river and frighten a fish.

GUIDE'S TIP If you are looking into a river from a high bank, try to blend in with any bankside cover so that you will not suddenly appear to a fish as a newly-planted tree trunk on the bank. You may need to get down on your hands and knees.

Reading the water The effects of wind on still waters

A strong wind blowing in the same direction over a body of water will start to "move" the water in the same direction. Nymphs, buzzers, and other forms of life will be blown along by the wind. The longer the wind blows in the same direction, the more pronounced will be the movement of water in the same direction as the wind. When the wind direction does change, the water movement will continue in the same direction for some time. It is important to check weather forecasts in the days before going fishing as well as for the day itself. If the wind direction has been changeable, where you start fishing will not be as obvious as if the wind has been steady for several days.

Wind influences fish and how they feed. Fish will tend to swim upwind, feeding as they go, before returning downwind at a greater depth and repeating the whole process. When casting to fish cruising upwind, it is important to cast far enough in front of them. If you don't give them enough "lead," your flies may be behind them before you realize it. If in doubt, cast further in front.

GUIDE'S TIP A short cast in difficult conditions to an area where there are fish will be much more profitable than a long one to an area where there are no fish.

Scum and wind lanes

These are a feature to target on any still water or lake. They are lines of flat water between the ripples and even (small) waves and usually start to appear once the water has started to warm up. They are always in line with the wind. Emerging insects that have difficulty breaking through the surface film get trapped in these calm areas, providing a floating restaurant for hungry trout. Boat anglers or anglers in a float tube will be able to fish more wind lanes than the bank angler as they do not always extend within casting range of the bank. Don't be tempted to drift down the middle of a scum or wind lane as fish will be able to see your boat in the calmer water. Keep to one side.

Feeding fish are often found in the "scum lanes" that develop on large lakes.

Currents

On windy days muddy water along the shore of a lake will show you where there are currents and undertows. Foam on the bank and muddy water will also show you where the wind has been blowing. A sharp boundary between the clean water—which trout prefer—and dirty water is likely to produce a good area of water to fish. Cast out so that your team of flies will fish slowly along the boundary line.

Still waters are never actually still and fish inhabit areas of a lake relative to these movements. It is important to be aware of these although other factors such as stocking policies and weed growth are equally relevant.

Whenever visiting a fishery, particularly an enclosed lake, always get up to date information. It can save hours of fruitless searching for fish.

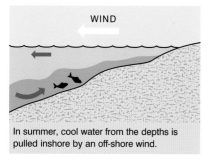

The movement of the water is often indicated by an area of colored water running out from the shore.

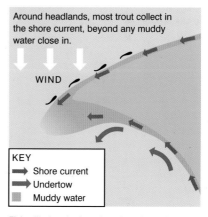

Fish will often be found on the edges of these colored areas.

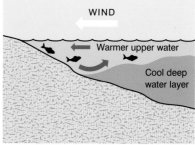

In summer, cool water from the depths is pulled inshore by an off-shore wind.

The temperature layers are directly affected by the wind. These drawings show how warmer water in winter may be found on the inshore wind bringing fish in very close, whereas in summer the opposite shore can be productive as it draws up the cooler water.

Reading the water Water temperature and air pressure

Summer

In high summer, when water temperatures are high and dissolved oxygen levels are low, all fish will seek areas where there is the maximum amount of oxygen available to them. This may mean fish going deep in still waters and reservoirs, finding cool water, a spring or a feeder stream, or riffles and turbulent stretches of rivers where there is that much more oxygen. Another place to find cool(er) water on still water is the windward shore, particularly if the wind direction has been constant for some days. This is because the wind will move the warm surface water downwind and, when it hits the lee shore, it will be pushed downward and will start to re-circulate—this will push cold water from deep down toward the surface on the windward shore. Fish the windward shore where the coolest water will be found.

Winter

At the other end of the scale, low temperatures mean low metabolism and that will mean fish eat less. Some fish in still waters may well be happy with a little fly rather than a large mouthful of a big lure. Rainbows are coldwater fish and can provide good sport in very cold weather.

Carrying a waterproof or fishing thermometer with you means that you can compare water and air temperatures. At the beginning and end of the year, winds that are warmer than the water will warm it slightly and attract fish to the lee shore. If the wind is really cold and therefore cooling the water, find a place to fish that is out of the wind. Once the temperature reaches about 45° F (7°C) fish will start moving and showing interest in food. But once the temperature hits about 70°F (21°C) fish will be reluctant to feed and insects reluctant to hatch.

Noting pressure

Fish are susceptible to changes in weather and the accompanying atmospheric pressure. They don't like change, and when the pressure rises or falls, they take time to adapt to the new pressure, often going off the feed before adapting to the changed conditions. Rising pressure foretells good weather, while a falling barometer means rain and probably wind as well. By noting and recording air pressure each time you go fishing you will be able to build up a picture of how air pressure affects your day's sport. After a while, this information will help you to decide when and where to fish and which flies and techniques to use.

Light penetration in water filters out colors differently. At greater depths things get more blue.

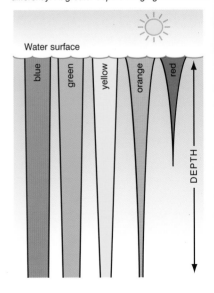

GUIDE'S TIP Are any flies hatching? Studying the
way fish are rising will tell you if they are taking nymphs
or flies on the surface. Rises to nymphs tend to be
marked by a boil or swirl in the water, without breaking
the surface, although the dorsal fin may be seen when
a fish is really high in the water.

Cold, wintery conditions do not necessarily mean poor sport. Check the barometer. If it is rising,
in any season, or if there is a prolonged spell of settled weather, prospects can be good. A falling
barometer tends to be the kiss of death at any time.

Reading the water Stop, look, and think before you cast

If you find it difficult to stop yourself starting fishing straight away without looking around, instead of rigging your rod and tying on a fly by your car, wait until you are at the waterside. Then, while you assemble your rod, fit the reel, and thread the line through the guides, keep your eyes and ears open. Look around and see if there are any birds swooping low over the waters which is a sure sign that flies are hatching; look to see if there are flies on the water and if fish are rising. If the answers to these questions are yes, then you should be looking for a suitable imitation in your dry fly boxes. If there are very few flies in the air and few, if any, fish rising, then a nymph, or other sub-surface fly will be the thing to go for.

Check conditions
Do you know which way the wind is blowing? Are you going to fish with the sun behind you so that your shadow falls on the water? Can you position yourself so that the sun helps you to see fish in the river? The little time to work out these things will be rewarded as soon as

you do start fishing because you will be standing in a position where you can see what is happening in the water, you won't be frightening fish unnecessarily and you are more likely to be using the right pattern of fly.

Be flexible
Don't assume that the same fly, or flies, presentation, and stretch of water are going to yield the same rewards today as they did yesterday or the last time that you fished. It's all too easy to get into a habit of simply doing the same thing every time you go fishing. Yes, you will catch fish but more by chance than because you have worked out what is happening and responded to the conditions and have chosen the best tactics to use. Fishing is a sport that rewards the thinking angler and the angler who has learnt to cope with a wide range of conditions.

At the riverside watch before you cast. Look for any signs that will indicate the presence of fish or what they are feeding on.

Time spent looking at the water and considering your approach is time well spent. Every day is different and conditions vary all the time. Don't have preconceived ideas!

Apart from anything else, fishing spots are usually great places to relax and contemplate the world.

Improve your catch rate on rivers Nymph fishing

One of the most difficult aspects of upstream nymphing is knowing when a fish has taken your fly. There are two reasons: One, takes can be very delicate, and second, a fish can reject your fly just as quickly as it takes it. Concentration is all important and your concentration will be helped if you have something to concentrate on.

Indicators

A small, subtle indicator is required, not something that is so big that it is, in effect, acting as a float. A small yarn or fluorescent putty indicator or a dry fly if you are fishing with two flies, is all that is needed. You want an indicator that you can watch and see when it reacts to something underwater. Not an indicator that suspends and controls the depth of your fly or flies.

The established, traditional indicator and way of spotting a take is to grease your leader well, including part of the tippet (how much depends on how deep you want your nymph to fish), and watching it for any sudden or strange

Nymphing on the Green River, Utah. Successful flies will include nymphs, but also terrestrial flies blown off the land such as ants and cicadas.

movement. The late English nymph expert Oliver Kite called the point where the end of the floating part of the leader pierces the water surface the dipping point. It was that point that he watched like a hawk. He was looking to see if the progress of the leader checked, moved, or swerved to one side or the other, dipped suddenly, or did anything

GUIDE'S TIP If you are having difficulty casting with spot-on accuracy to nymphing fish, try fishing with a stiffer leader. A soft leader suitable for delicate presentation of dry flies may lack the accuracy you need to place a nymph accurately.

Improve your techniques
and catch rate

unexpected—all signs of a take. Using a small indicator simply helps magnify those subtle movements and makes them easier to detect. Always expect a fish to take your fly and always set your hook when you see anything happen that might be a fish.

Observation

As well as watching your leader carefully, when you can see the fish you are trying to catch, watch if it moves toward your nymph, if you see the flash of white as it opens its mouth, or if it turns and follows your fly. If any of these things happen, set or be prepared to set your hook. Sometimes you will miss and hook the bottom or a fish. But if you don't you won't catch fish. Sometimes you will see your leader check, set the hook and think that you have caught a clump of weed. But every now and then that clump of weed will burst into life and a trout will rush off upstream, ripping line off your reel.

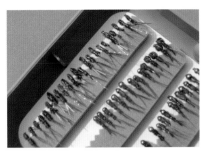

If in doubt, and with no other indication, start with general patterns such as a Gold Ribbed Hare's Ear or a Pheasant tail.

Fish spotting

Accurate casting can often make the difference between catching fish and failing to interest fish. A fish that can be seen moving about in the water, intercepting nymphs, first to the left and then to the right, will probably take your nymph as long as it drifts past where the fish expects them. But other fish will only show interest in an artificial nymph if it is placed with pin-point accuracy, so that it almost hits it on the nose.

Spotting takes while upstream nymphing is not easy. Strike gently at any suspicion of a take.

Improve your catch rate on rivers   199

Improve your catch rate on rivers Nymph fishing

GUIDE'S TIP Is the fish that you just saw rise holding where you think it is? Fish often follow a fly downstream before rising and eating it. That fish will then return upstream to its lie, waiting for the next fly along. If you cast to, or even just above the rise, you may well be casting downstream from the fish which is unlikely to see your fly.

Depth is critical

As well as casting accurately, you need
to judge how far upstream of a fish to
deliver your fly so that by the time it is
within range of your fish, your fly has sunk
to or is at the right depth. How far you
have to cast will depend on the speed of
flow of the water and the size and weight
of your fly. In some circumstances it may
be necessary to add a split shot to your
leader to get your fly down deep enough,
particularly in a big, powerful river.

Fishing out the cast

Always fish out your cast, as some fish
will follow your fly downstream before
taking it, or another fish that you might
not have seen will make a grab for your
fly. Keep an eye out for a fish that makes
a lunge for your fly just as you are about
to lift it from the river. What you are doing
is making an exaggerated induced take.
As you raise your rod to cast again,
you will make your nymph rise up in
the water like a natural swimming to
the surface to hatch. To a fish it is an
escaping morsel of food that must be
caught before it is lost.

*River fishing can vary from one extreme to
another and tactics have to be adjusted.*

The reward!

Improve your catch rate on rivers Dry fly fishing

In essence, dry fly fishing should be straightforward. You see a fish rise, you tie on a fly that matches the flies on the water, you cast upstream of where you saw the fish rise, wait as your fly floats downstream over the fish, which then rises up and takes your fly. You pause briefly as the fish turns down before setting the hook and then play and net your fish. Fortunately things are rarely that easy—at least for the angler who enjoys a challenge.

Fly choice

The first problem to deal with is choice of fly. Do you try to match the hatch or choose a generic attractor pattern? When you can see flies on the water and that fish are taking them, choosing an artificial is relatively straightforward. You would select a fly that is the right color, size, and profile. So-called "educated fish," particularly in heavily fished catch and release rivers where there are good, regular hatches of fly, are more likely to feed selectively. Here the correct choice of fly could be crucial. Fish in rivers where hatches are sparse or infrequent will feed opportunistically and will grab anything that they see that looks like a food item. Most of the time, a suitable attractor will succeed here.

Drag

Drag is the bug bear of river fishing, nowhere more so than dry fly fishing, but also subsurface when nymph fishing. Drag is caused by a number of factors, such as variations in strength and direction of currents across the width of a river. Some of the variations are more obvious than others. The only time that drag is beneficial and that you may want to create artificially, occurs when fishing a skating caddis pattern to imitate a natural running over the water to the bank.

Basic styles of dry fly and how they sit in the water. Note that all these sit in the surface film and not on top of the water. It is vital to get the fly to sit correctly or you will get lots of interest but few takes.

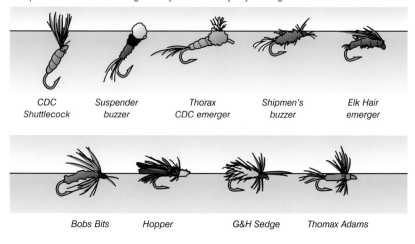

| CDC Shuttlecock | Suspender buzzer | Thorax CDC emerger | Shipmen's buzzer | Elk Hair emerger |

| Bobs Bits | Hopper | G&H Sedge | Thomax Adams |

You could try a number of strategies to overcome drag. Can you cast from a different position so that your line and/or leader does not cross different speed flows or crosses fewer? Will a long, softer leader that will land in a series of curves, coupled with a nice wavy cast, slow down the onset of drag? Can you mend your line so that your fly floats drag-free for that bit longer? An upstream mend will allow line and fly to drift at the same speed for longer before drag sets in. Can you cast more directly upstream, rather than across and up, so avoiding casting over different flow strengths? Time spent analyzing the problem and working out the best solution will be time well spent.

A midge at the point of hatching from its pupal case or shuck. Trout will feed on the pupa, the adult and the emerging fly, and they all can be imitated.

GUIDE'S TIP A prolific hatch of olives during the day is very likely to be followed by a heavy fall of spinners in the evening. During the evening look closely at the river and you should see spent flies lying on the surface.

Improve your catch rate on rivers Wading

Though careful wading will let you fish more water, wading badly could risk frightening fish. Wading a typical trout stream is a much more subtle and delicate business than wading in a big salmon or steelhead river where safety is a major concern. In rough, turbulent water you can get much closer to the fish than in a pellucid meadow stream. That, in part, is why short-line nymphing for grayling is so effective in mountain or fast-flowing rivers and streams. The fish cannot see very far in the turbulent water.

If you are going to wade a stretch of river, don't get straight into the water. Fish your way into the river and catch any fish that might be lying close to the bank, rather than wading straight in amongst them and frightening them. One frightened fish rushing off will, inevitably, frighten other fish, too.

Clumsy wading in a shallow stream will risk stirring up clouds of sand or silt perhaps to the detriment of an angler following you up the river, as well as

GUIDE'S TIP If you are having trouble seeing fish in a river, try bending down or moving so that the sun, if it is shining, is coming from a more helpful angle. Remember to look through the surface and into the water, not just at the surface.

damaging weeds and even killing bugs and small fish hiding in weed beds. When wading rocky rivers it is only too easy to make a lot of noise by scraping the studs on your wading boots on rocks or banging about with a wading stick. Do try to wade as quietly as possible.

Wading in fast water is dangerous. Footfalls are uncertain and a wading stick is essential. Remote rivers such as this one in South Africa are not likely to have emergency services on hand and you are very much on your own.

Wading improves an angler's understanding of the water, because it is closer and the angle of viewing is narrowed.

Improve your catch rate on reservoirs and still waters
The importance of the retrieve

There is more to fishing still waters or lakes than simply casting your fly, or team of flies, as far as you can and then pulling them back. How you pull them back, or retrieve them, is crucial. Retrieves vary in speed and style from the static retrieve to stripping line back as fast as you can, using both hands if necessary. The best known retrieve is undoubtedly the figure-eight. The retrieve and how it makes your flies perform in the water is fundamental to success.

Nymphing

Choice of retrieve will depend on conditions, what flies you are fishing, and if you are fishing sub-surface or dry flies on top. The figure-eight retrieve can be used to remove slack from the line before other retrieves are employed or as a retrieve in itself, at speeds varying from very slow to quick. It provides a smooth, jerk-free retrieve which can make a team of flies swim and move seductively.

Nymphs and buzzers seem to move very slowly but some are, for their size, quite speedy. Therefore, when fishing nymphs and buzzers, use the slowest retrieve possible—just inching the line

The figure-eight retrieve involves using the fingers to feed line into the hand slowly. It gives an even "nymphy" movement favored by nymph fishermen.

in—or even a static retrieve. Too fast a retrieve and your flies will appear to trout to be jet propelled. Tiny little pulls of maybe an inch of line at a time can be very effective. The static retrieve relies on removing any slack from the line immediately after casting and then leaving your line to its own devices. It will drift slowly with any surface currents or even be pushed by the wind, but there will be enough movement to impart a sense of life to your team of flies. Though some takes will be felt by holding the line between fingers and thumb, be prepared to set the hook at the slightest sign of movement from your line or leader.

Allowing your flies to sink between slow, steady pulls can be very effective. Pulls can be varied from very short to an armful of line and the time between pulls varied as well. Aim for an intermittent, erratic movement of your flies.

GUIDE'S TIP Don't be afraid to vary your speed and style of retrieve or mix and match different retrieves. If in doubt, try a slower retrieve or no retrieve at all, simply keeping in contact with your flies as they are moved by the wind or surface currents.

Pulling

For the energetic angler, there is a number of different high speed retrieves that can be employed. Names include ripping it back, the FTA (Fooling Them About), and the roly poly, when your rod is tucked under your arm and both hands are used to retrieve line in a smooth, continuous motion. What these retrieves suggest is that the angler should use their ingenuity to retrieve their flies in any way that they think will attract a hungry brown or rainbow trout.

By contrast lures are often stripped back with a full flow of the arm and sometimes at high speed.

A variation on this is the roly poly where overhand movements of the hands with the rod tucked under the arm cause the fly to return rapidly and at constant speed.

Improve your catch rate on reservoirs and still waters
Bank or boat

The decision to fish a still water or lake from the bank or a boat is often made for you on waters where there are no boats, or boat fishing is not allowed, and so the bank is the only choice. An alternative, again where allowed, is a float tube, which will give you the opportunity of getting afloat by yourself and without the need for a boat.

Casting into the wind
Fishing the lee shore from the bank and casting into the wind may seem as though you are trying to make things as hard as possible. Most anglers would assume that it is easier to cast with the

Float tubing allows the angler to get as close as it is possible to be. Avoid getting too comfortable though, and falling asleep!

wind behind you. The reason for fishing into the wind is that all the food will be blown toward you, the fish will be where the food is and, because the food and fish are close to the shore, you won't have to cast that far out.

Another advantage of fishing and casting into the wind is that you can achieve a very natural presentation of your fly, or flies, by simply retrieving at the same speed or even slower than the rate of wind drift.

Long casting
On many reservoirs and lakes the only reason for making a long cast is to give your flies time to get down to the right depth before they reach the "killing zone," which may be as close to the shore or bank as 30 or even 15 feet. Because fish can be feeding so close in, you must always fish-out your cast, right to the tip of your rod. If you retrieve and then lift off and cast again you may well have denied feeding fish sight of your flies, let alone the opportunity to feed on one.

Where the fish may not be close to the bank is on heavily fished small, still waters where there are anglers spaced around the water. The constant casting and movement on the bank will gradually push the fish into the middle of the water where they can feed undisturbed. This is a time when the angler who can cast furthest will be in with a chance of a fish or two.

The hang
The reason for marking your line is so that regardless of method of retrieve or line density, when you see the mark at the top ring, you will know exactly how

far away your flies are. Stop retrieving at that point for the first hang. Then continue the retrieve until the mark is at the reel. There are still three feet of fly line in the water. Stop again, wait and lift the rod: Don't retrieve the line. The top dropper fly will appear and that's the one you concentrate on hanging. Wait again and watch that fly. It's amazing how many fish come to that fly at that point. Not all will take it, and if you miss an offer, lift out and quickly whip the flies back into the water and let the flies sink. Often the fish will still be there and looking for the flies. Sometimes you'll get a pull on one of the other flies.

Once you have decided that there is nothing interested, lift your line off and recast. With long leaders, a quick roll or two usually gets enough line out of the rod to recast. And if for any reason you have pulled some of your leader through the tip top, a sideways sweep in the water will pull the line out again.

The "Hang" is a very effective method to use when boat fishing. Tackle is usually a 10-foot rod, a sinking line marked at 13 feet from the join with the leader and a two- or three-fly cast. The top dropper will often be a bushy or attractor fly, anything from a dabbler to a blob.

GUIDE'S TIP Try different casts, length of leader, weight of point fly and retrieve until you are sure that your point fly has actually reached the bottom. When it does, you will know that you are searching the full depth of water where you are fishing.

Improve your catch rate on reservoirs and still waters
Nymph fishing

Nymphs often hach out in the shallows. On dull days it is well worth exploring the edges of a still water.

Nymph fishing on still waters and lakes is all about fishing imitative patterns. You are fishing realistic, or suggestive, imitations of trout foods rather than big, aggressive patterns that will excite fish into grabbing a passing meal before it disappears. Nymphs are usually fished at a similar speed and depth to the naturals. Speed-wise, this often means very slowly.

Long leaders

When using a floating line to fish a very long leader—20 feet or more—it will often be necessary to ensure that you get your team of flies down to the bottom. A heavy nymph on the point will help a long leader to turn over as well as sink the flies on the droppers. When you have made your cast, straighten your line carefully and allow the leader to sink, which could take as much as two minutes or more.

When you are happy that your point fly is as deep as it can go, if there is a breeze allow it to take your line with it, or use a very slow hand retrieve to move your flies. Sometimes a combination of wind and retrieve is required. A floating line held under tension will cause your flies to lift slightly as it is blown by the wind.

If you are fishing a team of deep nymphs and you see signs of fish taking nymphs near the surface, you can respond to the change of tactic needed by changing your point fly. Instead of a heavy nymph, change it to something buoyant such as a muddler or floating fry pattern. This will mean that the end of your leader and the butt of your leader—remember to grease it—are on the surface, with the patterns on the droppers hanging just below the surface. This is known popularly as a "washing line."

An intermediate or sink-tip line can be used for fishing nymphs when it is impractical to fish a floating line, for example if there is a very strong cross wind that is blowing your line too quickly so that you loose control of your flies. The intermediate line will sink slowly so that you can fish just below the surface without the interference of the wind. You will not need to use such an extreme length of leader as you would with a floating line as the intermediate will follow your flies down toward the bottom, albeit very slowly.

In waters where fish feed on tiny midge pupae and small nymphs, slimly dressed "anorexic" nymphs will be the pattern of choice. They must be fished very slowly, often with a static retrieve. Superglue and Epoxy nymphs will sink quickly, even though tied without weight, because the glue or Epoxy stops air getting trapped in the dressing.

A drogue is useful when drifting in anything but the lightest breeze. It acts like a brake, slowing the boat down so that flies can be fished with more control. The standard attachment is a single, line placed centrally and adjusted with a G clamp to give a straight drift. Two point attachments though, allow the drogue to be retrieved without effort and from either end. Because it collapses as the boat is driven point forward, it can be left, with care, in the water as the boat is driven to the top of the next drift.

Improve your catch rate on reservoirs and still waters
Dry fly fishing

When fish start rising visibly to flies on the surface and you decide to fish dry flies, you should change your leader from a buzzer/nymph leader to a dry fly one. The leader should be shorter, about 14 feet, with a dropper at 6 feet and the point fly a further 8 feet from the top end, and made from any mono other than fluorocarbon, which might sink tiny dries. A shorter, simpler leader will make it much easier to cast accurately to rising fish and to target cruisers. Good turnover and presentation are needed when fishing dries.

Making flies float and leaders sink

Dry flies will need to be well "greased" to make sure that they stay afloat for what will often be a long time, particularly in comparison to river fishing. When greasing your fly, or flies, take care not to get any floatant on your leader, which you want to sink just below the surface to reduce its visibility. To reduce the chance of the leader sinking a tiny dry, apply a tiny amount of grease to the leader just by the fly. When a lake is flat and calm, a greased, floating leader on the surface will be very visible because it will distort

GUIDE'S TIP The longer your flies remain on the surface, the more chance fish will have to find them. Fish a cast slowly and methodically and try not to be distracted by fish rising and the temptation to cast to each and every one of them.

A big splashy rise might indicate a feeding fish at the surface. It is important to be able to distinguish the types of rise and know when fish are feeding and what on.

the surface film, which is why you want it to sink just below the surface. If your leader refuses to sink, then treat it with a sinking compound.

Spotting takes

If your flies are small and not very easy to see, the way to make sure that you don't miss a possible take is to look along your fly line and beyond the visible tip to the area where your flies will be, and if a fish rises anywhere along that line, set the hook. You must assume that any fish moving along that line is after your fly. If you find that your flies have sunk, don't just heave them out of the water so that you can dry them but retrieve them with a figure eight retrieve. You may well catch a fish, which might suggest that you should be fishing sub-surface.

Fishing two flies allows the angler to fish either two dry flies of different patterns, or a dry and an emerger. If fishing with a dry and an emerger, you

can vary the depth at which the emerger fishes by fishing it either on the point or on the dropper. An emerger fished as the point fly will sink deeper than on the dropper when it will be held higher in the water by the dry fly on the point, particularly if that is a bushy buoyant pattern. The dry fly will also act as an indicator and will signal a take to the sunk emerger.

Terrestrial insects blown on to the water, such as this daddy longlegs, can set off feeding spells.

Improve your catch rate
for salmon Water temperature

When fishing for Atlantic salmon, water temperature is more important than with almost any other game fish. Some anglers maintain that 42°F (5°C) is a crucial temperature while others go for a slightly higher figure. When the water is colder salmon will not run far up a river and will be reluctant to attempt to ascend waterfalls and weirs in their path. But once water temperatures reach the mid to high 40s, say 48° F (9°C), then fish will start to run and show interest.

Hot summer days and low water levels mean high temperatures in rivers. When the thermometer shows temperatures of about 66°F (19°C), salmon are likely be too lethargic to show much, if any, interest in your fly.

Temperature and depth

Temperature affects fishing methods and optimum times. When the water temperature is below 48°F (9°C) big flies fished deep will be the order of the day. But in the winter or spring, as the air temperature rises during the day, it will be possible to fish higher in the water. A small increase in water temperature may well encourage a fish to take a fly. If there is a lot of extra water in the river, even when the temperature has risen, it may still be necessary to use a sinking line to keep your fly deep. But come summer and warmer water, small flies can be fished close to or even in or on the surface.

As the fish will be lying deep in cold water, you must get your fly down to their depth. This means fishing a large, heavy fly on a full sinking line. Fishing a full sinking line and a heavy brass tube fly will certainly ensure that you are fishing deep, but this will create serious problems when you want to make another cast. Before you can make a Spey cast, you have to get the line back up to the surface. And the only way that you can do this is by a series of energetic, energy-sapping roll casts, assuming that your line is too deep to bring to the surface by simply raising your rod tip. Another way to get your line to the surface—it is particularly effective with a sink tip—is to use a cast that has a powerful start, which will lift the line up in the water. A good cast is the snap T, or a snake roll.

Interchangeable tips

Interchangeable sink tips are less expensive than having to buy a range of different lines, and the accompanying spools or extra reels, and they can be changed quickly and easily without having to reel in the line in use and then re-string the new line. Interchangeable tips range from floaters to very fast sinkers. To get really deep, you can even fish two sink tips looped-to-looped to each other. It is better to use a heavier line or sink tip to get deep than rely on fishing an even bigger and heavier fly.

GUIDE'S TIP If you don't want to use a lot of roll casts to raise a sunk line when fishing cold rivers, use an interchangeable sink tip. The right sink tip will get your fly to the required depth and casting will be easier because the majority of the casting part of your line will be floating.

Improve your catch rate
for salmon Floating lines

Some anglers may think that fishing sinking lines and big, heavy flies is too much like hard work. Fishing floating lines in warm weather in lower water will be a pleasure in comparison. Once water temperatures are permanently above 48°F (9°C), then the floating line with small flies comes into its own, particularly in summer when grilse (one sea-winter fish) return to the river of their birth. Shorter and lighter rods can be used as well, though long leaders will be required as good presentation is much more important.

Perfect presentation on a breezy day when the surface of the river is well ruffled is not always necessary, but as soon as the river is calm, then trout-style presentations will be advantageous. Here a long, tapered leader will help and the fine point will allow small flies to swim naturally.

GUIDE'S TIP If the water level is low then you can use a slow sinker or sink tip line. But once the water temperature is above 50°F you should change to a floating line.

Improve your catch rate in saltwater Fishing with a guide

If you are fishing with a guide, listen to what he tells you to do and act on his advice. A good guide will know the waters that you are fishing and will be doing all that he can to give you the best day's sport. A saltwater guide spotting shoals of fish from his poling platform has all the advantages over his client. Guides are used to the light conditions, they know what they are looking for and, above all, they have the added advantage of height.

To give yourself the best chance of seeing fish when your guide tells you a shoal is coming within casting range, equip yourself with a pair of good quality Polaroid glasses to reduce glare and make it easier to see fish. A cap with a long peak will help keep the sun out of your eyes. It will take a while to get your eye in and know what you are looking for. Fish everywhere, in salt or fresh water, have the ability to blend in with their surroundings, making them that little bit more difficult to spot—and few do it better than bonefish.

GUIDE'S TIP The best bonefishing spots are often remote and it is important to take all you will need with you.

Saltwater

While you are talking to your guide, before you start, do ask him where he is taking you and, more important, why. This is the best way of slowly building your own knowledge base that you can tap into and use on future trips. Often a guide is only necessary for the first couple of days of a trip.

Quick, accurate casting is the order of the day. Spend some time before a saltwater trip practicing casting with the rod and flies that you will be fishing. If you can do this on a windy day, so much the better. And don't forget to spend as much time as possible practicing casting into the wind.

Guides world wide can be invaluable if one is unfamiliar with the water. Precise location of fish is a major problem when traveling to new places, and a good local guide can get you on the fish with the correct techniques very quickly.

Because fishing conditions can be extreme with hot sun, salt water (obviously) and super-hard-fighting fish that will show-up any weaknesses in your tackle, do take a spare rod, reel, spool, and line (or even lines) so that you can re-equip yourself as and when necessary. You don't want to lose time on the water through a tackle failure. Do make sure to wash all your tackle in fresh water at the end of each day.

There are hot spots on the flats the same as there are in rivers and on lakes. While your guide should know them all, tell-tale signs to look out for include bird activity over feeding areas, surface disturbances however slight and clouds of sand that have been produced by feeding fish. Fish that create sand clouds as they feed are more easy to approach as they won't be able to see you so easily.

Bonefishing check list

- *Rods: 9ft #7/8, 9ft #8/9 and spinning rod*
- *Reels with floating and intermediate saltwater lines*
- *Sunglasses*
- *Sandals or light shoes*
- *Flashlight*
- *Digital camera and spare chip, with battery charger and batteries*
- *Underwater camera*
- *Thermometer*
- *Reel lubrication and tool kit*
- *Laminated tide table and creek map*
- *Fly tying materials and vise*
- *Leader material*
- *Wading boots and socks*
- *Hats and caps*
- *Mains plug travel adaptor*
- *Medical kit*
- *Insect repellent and bite cream*
- *Sun cream*
- *Wading waist bag*
- *T-shirts, shirts, shorts, and pants*
- *Flight tickets and passport*
- *Driving licence*
- *Local currency*

A guide on a flat boat not only puts the boat in the right area, but stands on a special platform and spots fish for his client to cast to.

Pike tactics
In rivers and lakes

Fly fishing for pike is challenging, exciting, rewarding, and not without its dangers. The first time that you see a pike rush out like a torpedo from among bankside reeds in a lake or from under a river bank will make your heart miss a beat! And when one follows your fly slowly as you retrieve it and you look down to see a pair of cold, malevolent eyes staring up at you before it turns and slips away into the deep, the appeal of doing battle with these large predators can be irresistible.

A pike's mouth is full of rear-facing teeth that are sharper than a razor. Never try to unhook a pike with your fingers—keep them well away from those teeth. Wear gloves and always use a pair of needle-nose pliers or a pair of forceps (hemostats) to unhook a pike, and always use barbless hooks.

This is typical pike water, where the bend of a river creates a break in the flow creating slack areas and eddies. Places where pike can lie in wait for quarry using the minimum of energy.

Where to find pike

Pike are very widespread and many anglers will have easy access to suitable waters. Pike are even caught all around the shores of the Baltic where the water is brackish. You can stalk pike where the water is clear and shallow. Watch for shoals of small fish jumping out of the water in panic as they try to get away from a marauding pike.

The time of year, air, and water temperatures all play a key role in where you are likely to find fish. In Swedish and other northern lakes in the summer they are to be found lurking in the reedy shallows, under or close to water lilies, lying in ambush for any unwary small fish that makes the mistake of swimming

GUIDE'S TIP When unhooking a pike, hold the fish firmly behind its eyes with one hand and, with the other, take hold of the bend of the hook and carefully twist it out of the pike's jaw. Use pliers, particularly for a fish hooked inside its mouth.

within range. They will also "lurk" in rivers, tucked away and often out of sight under cutaway banks. At other times they can be seen in mid-stream where you can stalk them.

In winter pike don't need to feed so much as their metabolism is very slow. Fish deep and slow in areas where a pike can lie out of the current and little energy has to be used to stay on station. At any time of the year it will pay to try different retrieves—particularly varying the speed—until you find one that works.

Lines and leaders

Generally a floating line will be all that you need but a sink tip, or intermediate, could be useful if you need to get your fly down deep. A good quality reel suitable for the line weight is all that is needed. You don't need a saltwater reel of the quality that you would for bonefish or tarpon. A good pike reel must have a good drag with low start-up inertia. Pike may not make long runs but they do make fast and powerful runs.

Leaders should be short and strong and with a powerful taper capable of turning over big, bulky flies. Special pike

leaders are readily available or you can use the thick end of a braided leader, with a ring on the end to which you attach the wire trace.

You don't need lots of equipment for a pike fishing session: A small bag with the flies, forceps, gloves, and other accessories, then a rod, reel, and landing net. Travel light and explore the likely areas.

> **GUIDE'S TIP** A short wire tippet is essential to protect your leader from a pike's vicious teeth. Pike are even capable of making a mess of wire so do keep an eye on your tippet and be prepared to replace it if it is showing signs of wear and damage.

Conservation
Catch and release

More anglers practice "catch and release" today, either voluntarily because they feel that it is the right thing to do or by necessity when fishing catch and release waters. This means that on heavily fished rivers, fish are going to be caught and released many times during the season. If they are to survive—which is the objective of catch and release—they must be handled properly at all stages from the initial hook set through to the release.

Unhooking

When fish are hooked and being played, they suffer the effects of a build-up of lactic acid. The longer you play a fish the bigger the build-up of lactic acid, and when you come to release the fish, the longer it will take to recover as it disperses the acid. It is best to fish with tackle that will allow fish to be played and released quickly, without undue battle. You don't want to play fish to death. Fish that are less tired will recover more quickly and will have a much better chance of survival when released.

A still-lively, lightly hooked fish will shake itself free if you hold the hook firmly, either with your fingers or a pair of forceps. Releasing a fish this way does mean that you won't be able to hold it while it recovers. When it is necessary to hold a fish to unhook it, or in the water while it recovers, always wet your hands first as holding a fish with a dry hand will remove some of the protective slime from its body.

Forceps can be used to remove hooks as well as special catch and release tools such as the Ketchum Release. You should always have one or the other with you as you cannot rely on always being able to get hold of the fly with your fingers.

Releasing

Hold it in the water while it recovers, facing into the flow, making sure that its gills are free to function properly. If you want to move it about, push it forward and round in a circle. Don't push it forward and then pull it backward. You want water, and thus oxygen, to go into its mouth. All fish will take longer to recover in the summer when water temperatures are very high. You should always make sure that any fish you release does, in fact, swim off. If a fish seems sluggish or simply sits on the bottom, a gentle nudge with the tip of your rod or a toe will usually wake it up, unless it is still completely exhausted. If that is the case, keep an eye on the fish until you see it swim off.

GUIDE'S TIP When photographing a fish, keeping it in or close to the water will reduce the likelihood of injury if it should kick or struggle and fall from your hands.

Don't lift a fish out of the water until the cameraman is ready. Ideally, try to keep as much of it as possible in the water. Hold a big fish with one hand round the root of its tail and use the other to cradle its weight behind its gills. Don't squeeze or grip it hard as you may rupture its internal organs.

Diseases

As more and more anglers travel to fish different rivers and lakes, not only within their home countries but increasingly visiting foreign destinations, the likelihood of them unwittingly transferring diseases from one country or river system to another can only increase. It is up to each and every angler to be vigilant and take all reasonable precautions to prevent the spread of potentially ruinous diseases.

Glossary

Aberdeen Hook A strong style of hook, often linked with sea fishing.

Albright Knot A very good and reliable knot for joining two lines of very different thicknesses or materials.

Ally's Shrimp A very effective salmon shrimp fly developed by Alastair Gowans.

Arbor The part of a fly reel that holds the fly line. Also known as the spool.

Attractor An artificial fly designed to attract fish rather than represent a natural food item.

Backing (e.g. Dacron, gel-spun or micro) Thin line attached to the reel arbor and then the fly line to provide extra line if a fish makes a long run, and to increase the diameter of the arbor so the fly line is stored in larger coils.

Backing Knot A knot used to attach the backing to the arbor or spool of a fly reel.

Blue Charm A popular pattern of sea trout and salmon fly, originally fully dressed. Dates back to the 1800s.

Bob's Bits A stillwater dry fly pattern designed by Bob Worts. Tied in various colors it can be fished to represent different naturals.

Booby A buoyant fly with two foam "boobs" at the head.

Buzzers (e.g. Epoxy Buzzer) An artificial version of a midge pupa.

Caddis fly A roof-winged fly of the family trichoptera. A very important source of food for trout as there are hundreds of different caddis around the world.

CDC Shuttlecock A dry pattern tied with a bunch of extremely buoyant CDC feathers. CDC is *cul de canard*, which are the feathers from around the preen gland of a duck.

Clear line A colorless line designed for stealthy presentations.

Clinch Knot Popular knot for tying a fly to the tippet.

Diawl Bach Originally a Welsh nymph pattern that means Little Devil, now very popular on stillwaters.

Dipping Point The point at which the leader cuts through the surface of the water when fishing nymphs upstream.

Down locking reel seat A seat, or reel fixing, that positions the reel nearest the butt-end of the rod.

Dropper An extension of a section or length of leader used to attach extra fly or flies to a leader, or sometimes one fly to the hook bend of another

Dry fly (e.g. Thorax Adams) A fly that is fished dry and floating on the surface of the water.

Dun (*See* Sub-imago) A fully-emerged sub-adult mayfly.

Emerger An artificial fly that represents a nymph as it is hatching.

False cast A cast used to extend line or dry a fly, as opposed to a cast that presents the fly to a feeding fish.

Fish-finder An electronic device with a screen that shows the location of fish and underwater features.

Floatant A synthetic liquid or paste used to treat dry flies dry to stop them sinking.

FTA (Fooling Them About) An aggressive stillwater retrieve used to tease or antagonize fish into taking a fly.

Garry A pattern of salmon fly, with either feather or hair wing.

G & H Sedge An artificial caddis, or sedge, pattern developed by John Goddard and Cliff Henry.

Hairwing fly Any artificial fly with wings made out of animal hair as opposed to feathers.

Hatch-matcher An artificial fly specifically selected to match flies that are hatching and that trout are feeding on.

Hemostat Also known as surgical clamps or forceps and used to extract flies and hooks from a fish's jaw.

Hopper Grasshopper or an artificial fly with a resemblance to the crane fly and similar terrestrials.

Lanyard Length of line used to secure a wading stick to an angler's belt or vest.

Leader A (usually) tapered extension to the fly line to which a tippet is attached.

Leader clipper Similar to nail clippers used to trim tag ends of knots in leaders and tippets typically when changing fly patterns.

Muddler (e.g. Muddler Minnow) A fly, with a shaped deer hair head, tied by Don Gapen in 1937 to represent a sculpin or minnow.

Nail Knot Knot used to attached butt section of a leader to the fly line.

Piggy's tail A series of tight twists in the end of the tippet when the knot has slipped.

Pike line A fly line with a heavy or steep taper that will turnover large wind-resistant flies.

Poppers High floating, buoyant flies popular for catching largemouth bass and northern pike.

Saltwater line A fly line with a taper designed to turn-over often bulky flies and surface coating suitable to withstand the rigors of use in salt water.

Scandinavian Shooting Head System Shooting head fly line system developed in Scandinavia for fishing with double hand rods.

Scud Small, shrimplike freshwater crustacean.

Scum lane A line of bubbles along the direction of the wind often inhabited by fish feeding on flies trapped in the surface film.

Shipman's Buzzer An imitation of an adult midge designed by Dave Shipman.

Sinkant A "potion" applied to a leader or tippet to make it sink.

Sinking line Fly line that is designed to sink available in different sink rates.

Sink tip Fly line with a tip that sinks, ideal for fishing sub surface.

Snake roll A cast used to change direction more quickly than using a double spey cast.

Snap T A popular cast when fishing with sink tip lines often used by West Coast steelhead anglers.

Stoat's Tail A salmon fly tied originally with hairs from a stoat's tail.

Streamer A wet fly or lure tied with long flowing materials.

Sub-imago A newly-hatched upwing mayfly, the penultimate stage of development.

Suspender Buzzer An artificial midge (chironomid) pattern designed to hang vertically in the surface film.

Taper (e.g. WF and DT) All fly lines are designed and manufactured with a taper and are named after the type and location of the taper.

Thorax CDC emerger An artificial emerger pattern tied with CDC.

Tippet A length of sacrificial level mono between the fly and the end of the main leader.

Trilene Knot A strong and reliable knot used to tie a fly to a tippet.

Up locking reel seat A seat, or reel fixing, that positions the reel nearest the bottom of the rod handle and so away from the butt end of the rod.

Washing line A method of presenting a team of flies in the feeding zone very naturally, usually with at least one buoyant fly at the end of the leader.

Weed guard A length of thick mono tied to a fly hook to prevent it snagging in weeds.

Wind lane A calm strip of water alongside an area of water rippled by the wind.

Zinger A pin-on reel with an extendable leash used to attach tools and other accessories of equipment to a fishing vest.

Zonker A strip of typically rabbit fur used to tie streamers or lures which are then known as zonkers.

Index

Acknowledgments

Alamy: p.156 b IMAGEiN/Alamy; p.163 Jeffrey S. Adams/Alamy; p.218 b Mark Boulton/Alamy. Corbis: p.13 Buddy Mays/Corbis; p.134 Christopher Cormack/Corbis.

Getty Images: p.1 Tom Montgomery/Aurora/Getty Images; p.6 Burton McNeely/The Image Bank/Getty Images; p.16 Tom Montgomery/Aurora/Getty Images; p.130/131 John Kelly/Riser/Getty Images; p.139 b David Epperson/Photographer's Choice/Getty Images; p.152 t Dan Ham/Riser/Getty Images; p.173 b Brian Bailey/Taxi/Getty Images; p.196 David Epperson/Photographer's Choice/Getty Images; p.199 t Karl Weatherly/Photographer's Choice/Getty Images; p.200 Tom Montgomery/

Aurora/Getty Images; p.201 Hans Pfletschinger/Science Faction/Getty Images; p.210 Burton McNeely/The Image Bank/Getty Images; p.211 t Whit Richardson/Aurora/Getty Images; p.213 Karl Weatherly/Photodisc/Getty Images.

Chris McLeod: p.141, p.146, p.150 b, p.154 t, p.155 l, p.156 t, p.165 cr, p.166 r, p.171 both, p.174 l, p.177 c & b, p.178 tr, p.190.

Cliff Waters: p.11, p.127, p.132, p.133, p.136, p.144 b, p.148, p.150 l, p.151, p.153 r, p.155 b, p.157 b, p.160, p.165 cl, p.167 br, p.169, p.170 b, p.174 r both, p. 175 cr, p.176, p.177 t, p.178 b, p.179, p.182 both, p.183 tl, p.185 t, p.195 t, p.198, p.199 b, p.205 all, p.207, p.208, p.209, p.211 b, p.217.

Mike Murphy: p.170 t, p.187 b.

Sean Cutting: p.8/9, p.10 b, p.137 l, p.143 t, p.168, p.189 b, p.204, p.215.

Snowbee, used with kind permission: p.128, p.135, p.137 r, p.138, p.140 both, p.142, p.147 all, p.149, p.164 tr & bl, p.165 tr, p.167 tl, p.173 c.

Terry Lawton: p.10 t, p.12, p.14/15, p.130, p.139 tl & tr, p.143 b, p.144 t, p.153 l, p.157 t, p.162 all, p.164 br, p.165 b, p.166 l, p.167 tr, p.167 bl, p.172, p.173 t, p.175 all, p.178 tl, p.183 bl cr br, p.185 b both, p.186, p.187 t, p.188 both, p.189 t, p.193, p.194, p.195 b, p.197 all, p.202, p.203, p.206 both, p.214, p.216, p.218 t & c, p.219 both, p.220, p.221 both